RELIGIOUS VALUES OF THE TERMINALLY ILL

A HANDBOOK FOR HEALTH PROFESSIONALS

RELIGIOUS VALUES OF THE TERMINALLY ILL

A HANDBOOK FOR HEALTH PROFESSIONALS

by:

Delfi Mondragón, Editor
Department of Health Science
New Mexico State University
Las Cruces, New Mexico

© 1997
by The University of Scranton Press

All rights reserved

Library of Congress Cataloging-in-Publication Data

Religious values of the terminally ill : a handbook
  for health professionals / by Delfi Mondragón,
  editor.
        p. cm.
    Includes index.
    ISBN 0–940866–64–1
    1. Terminal care--Religious aspects. 2. Ter-
minally ill--Religious life. 3. Death--Religious
aspects. I. Mondragón, Delfi, 1941–
R726.8.R44   1997
291.1'7832175--dc21   97–16793
                                            CIP

Marketing and Distribution
University of Scranton Press
Chicago Distribution Center
11030 S. Langley
Chicago   IL   60628

PRINTED IN THE UNITED STATES OF AMERICA

TABLE OF CONTENTS

PREFACE

espect for human dignity has long been heralded as the overarching principle that should guide the relationship between professionals and the people who seek their services. However, the challenge of exactly how to effect this laudable goal is elusive, especially as professionals come into contact with an increasingly rich mix of people from all parts of the world who seem to differ significantly from the professionals themselves in their beliefs, habits, and lifestyles. One constructive response to this dilemma has been to create educational experiences geared to sensitizing professionals and future professionals to differences. "Diversity" has become a byword in American society. The focus of most of this activity has been on gender, ethnicity, social class and, to a lesser extent, sexual preference. There has been remarkably little focus on differences in religious and other belief systems and how those factors impact the type and quality of life.

As we approach the millennium, an explicit focus on religious belief, and particularly how belief translates to practice in important life situations, must be brought fully into the consideration of good patient care in the health professions context. Under the direction of Dr. Delfi Mondragón, a conference was created to begin redressing this negligence. She chose the focus of how to treat dying persons and the handling of the dead body. The enthusiastic responses from participants and faculty alike were indicators that there is a felt need for more insight, understanding, and exchange of ideas at a very practical level.

The purpose of this book, an enlarged and edited version of the papers presented at the conference, is to provide one important vehicle for further discussion and reflection. We believe it will serve that end, thereby contributing significantly to the goal of learning how to show respect for persons in one of their most intensely human situations.

Ruth Purtilo, Ph.D., Director
Center for Health Policy & Ethics
Creighton University
1996

INTRODUCTION

A t the Creighton University Center for Health Policy and Ethics, as well as in the Saint Joseph Hospital Ethics Committee, we are frequently asked by pastoral care clergy questions such as, "How does one deal with a Muslim patient who is dying?" Similarly, nurses will ask, "What are the principles that we should know to be supportive with a Buddhist patient who has been diagnosed with a terminal illness?" Further, with the emerging climate of managed care, hospitals and physician groups who are in the process of signing managed care contracts with Indian nations have asked us how to deal in a culturally sensitive fashion with patients of a given Indian tribe. As we work with Indian tribes we discover, further, that tribal councils of Indian nations declare that they expect health care providers to give culturally relevant health care, if the tribe is to sign a managed care contract.

As our country becomes more racially and ethnically diverse, it also becomes more diverse in religions. Health care and pastoral care providers want to be supportive of all, and particularly dying patients, but frequently feel uneducated about specific cultural groups and their value systems. Further, the General Congregation, 34, of the Society of Jesus, speaking on "Our Mission and Inter-religious Dialogue" (Interim Documents, 1.1.3), guides and directs,

> "Indigenous religions and the great world religions, the new religious movements and the fundamentalist groups invite us to a dialogue that is proper to the perspective and challenge of each."

and concludes,

> "As Companions of Jesus sent into today's world, a world characterized by religious pluralism, we have a special responsibility to promote inter-religious dialogue."

For these reasons, we at the Center for Health Policy and Ethics, who co-labor with the Society of Jesus, decided in late 1995 to bring together members familiar with the spiritual values of the Omaha and Winnebago Indian tribes, the Zen Buddhists, the Jewish faith, the Islamic faith and the Nation of Islam, and the Jehovah's Witnesses to explain to us their relevant values in acute illness and death. We would do this for our seventh annual hospital ethics committee workshop. Our goal was to create a forum for knowledgeable leaders to teach pastoral care professionals, physicians, nurses, medical social workers, and others about the values and norms in their religious traditions, in order to facilitate these professionals' communication with patients in times of serious acute and chronic illness and death.

Further, we would distribute the written papers, reflecting or expanding their oral presentation. The speakers were given guidelines and questions to be answered: a general overview of the history, demography, or highlights of their (group or) religion, then answers to the following considerations:

1. The perspective of the religion on the meaning of illness and suffering.
2. The view of the religion on the value of suffering.
3. The view of the group on afterlife and its meaning.
4. The key terms and vocabulary that nurses, physicians, and clergy might use in dealing with a patient and his family at times of acute illness and death.
5. Where to call for assistance when physicians, nurses, social workers, or hospital clergy need information about dealing with patients of the religion, particularly if they are acutely ill or dying.

6   What is the view of the religion on visiting the sick?

7.   If death occurs, what is the religion's practice regarding the postmortem attention of the body?

Given the cost of offering an all-day workshop, the decreasing budgets of health care programs, and our wish to involve as many care providers as possible, we applied for a mini-grant from the Nebraska Humanities Council.   The council requested letters of recommendation from health care and humanities leaders. It was at this point, reading the letters, that we truly began to understand the value of what we were doing. The letters spoke of the significance: A senior physician wrote,

> "I served on the . . . Ethics Committee, and I know that among the many thorny problems with which we had to wrestle, sensitivity to and adequate reaction to different faith perspectives on medical issues would have been among those at the forefront. . . . more and more attention needs to be given to such issues."

A Jesuit priest and director of hospital pastoral care wrote,

> "This program . . . is crucial in the present environment of health care reform. With shorter hospital stays, . . . and a general

decrease in the amount of time allowed for contact between care givers and patients, we face the enormous challenge of maintaining the most deeply human aspects of healing and preparation for death while having less time and fewer resources. . . . Having a deeper familiarity with the cultural and religious context of each patient and family will help us to enter more quickly and fully into their experience of illness, suffering, and death."

A college dean of arts and sciences wrote,

"There are many of us who feel strongly about the critical need for education to promote understanding of cultural, ethnic, and religious diversity. [The workshop] is particularly relevant to us in Nebraska since the major [Indian] tribes and the Black Muslims will be invited to make major presentations."

We received the grant from the Nebraska Humanities Council. We are grateful to the council and to the writers of the letters. It required time and much networking to find credible speakers, particularly for the Native American tribes' religions. We were sensitive to the recent trend of "instant experts" in teaching, for example, healing practices. We therefore verified both expertise and character, especially with elders, before engaging the speakers.

The final lineup with their respective biographies were:

Rosalee Thomas is a member of the Winnabago Tribe of Nebraska. A licensed clinical social worker and mental health practitioner, she is the director of Mental Health and Social Services at the Carl T. Curtis Health Education Center for the Omaha tribe of Nebraska and Iowa. She has lectured extensively on Winnabago Indian culture.

Rudi Mitchell has been tribal council chairman of the Omaha Tribe of Nebraska and Iowa. He also holds a doctoral degree in education and a master's degree in social work. He has worked extensively with Indian Health Service and several Indian tribes. He speaks today of the Omaha tribe's perspectives.

Kyoki Roberts is a Zen Buddhist priest and meditation teacher. Rev. Roberts' lineage of priests consists of eighty-three priests, all male; she is the first female priest. She began her training in 1987, and continues to train with Nonin Chowaney at the Nebraska Zen Center. She completed monastic training at Zuio-ji and Shogo-ji Monasteries in Japan. She is certified to teach by the Soto Zen Church in Japan. She now serves as priest at Nebraska Zen Center in Omaha.

Naeem Muhammud is an Imam, or priest, in the classic Islamic tradition. He is affiliated with

Massid Das Al-Islam. His approach is based on the Holy Prophet's teachings and the Koran. He will speak of the classic Islamic view of illness and death, including funeral preparation and afterlife.

Brother Melvin X is a minister in the Black Muslim Islamic tradition. He is educated and experienced in the process of the Nation of Islam. This approach is based upon facts as well as historical data and prayer. Brother Melvin addresses the Black Muslim perspectives of illness and death.

Leonard Greenspoon holds a doctorate in religious studies and the Klutznick Chair in Jewish Civilization at Creighton University. He has been a professor of religion since 1980 and is a scholar of Bible translation and archeology. He will approach the historical, theological, and sociological aspects that point to traditional Jewish beliefs and practices and how these have been modified in recent times. He will stress the diversity, as well as the communality, of the Jewish people.

Ronald Rieckman of the Jehovah's Witnesses Hospital Liaison Committee has received training at the headquarters of Jehovah's Witnesses and is an elder in the church. He will relate and explain beliefs surrounding illness and death in patients of the Jehovah's Witness faith.

Other key people involved were James Clifton, S.J., Director of Pastoral Care, St. Joseph Medical

Center, and Richard Hauser, S.J., professor of theology, who has written extensively on illness and suffering in the Catholic perspective, who summarized the empirical and theoretical points, respectively. Ruth Purtilo, Ph.D., director of the Center for Health Policy and Ethics, and Delfi Mondragón, Dr.P.H., project director and editor of this work, were both present throughout the day.

The eighty-six workshop attendees were members of pastoral care—clergy and laypeople, social workers, physicians, and nurses. They were delighted with the material presented by the members of various religious faiths. They, and other professionals unable to attend, encouraged us to publish these papers as a reference book or for general knowledge for health care and pastoral care providers in hospitals.

In addition to the religious faiths listed, and for which we had elicited papers, we felt strongly, and the evaluations verified, that Hinduism and Seventh-Day Adventists and two additional Native American tribes should be included, because of the size of the tribe—increasing the probability that hospitals would admit them—or because of the extreme difference of their values around illness and death. These two tribes were the Plains Indians and the Navajo nation. These four papers were commissioned following the workshop, and the writers were given the same guidelines of questions.

Additionally, in discussing the cultural variance of reactions around serious illness and death, it was pointed out to the editor that Hispanic Americans in the Southwest U.S. and their families reacted quite differently from others. To the editor this was the norm, and she began to explain the rationale and value. At this point colleagues challenged her to write a chapter on this group, and to address the same questions. The challenge was accepted. The writers of this second set of papers were:

Milton L. Perry, currently a pastor at the Golden Hills Seventh-Day Adventist Church in Bellevue, Nebraska. Dr. Perry received his B.A. in theology from Loma Linda University, his M.Div. from the Seventh-Day Theological Seminary at Andrews University, and his Ph.D. from Baylor University. He has taught in a church-related school for two years and served as an active pastor for 18 years.

Debasis Bagchi is a Hindu Brahmin, and currently chairs the Religious Committee of the Hindu Temple in Omaha, Nebraska. He is a research associate professor in the Department of Pharmaceutical and Administrative Sciences at Creighton University School of Pharmacy & Allied Health Professions. He holds a doctoral degree and his research interests include mechanism of toxicity induced by environmental pollutants, pesticides, and heavy metals, and design of novel antioxidant drugs.

Marlene EchoHawk holds a master's degree in

guidance and counseling and a doctorate in psychology. Her tribal affiliation is with the Otoe-Missouria tribe. Presently, she is the deputy chief of the Alcoholism and Substance Abuse Program Branch at Indian Health Service Headquarters West, in Albuquerque, New Mexico. She has held various clinical and administrative positions, and has served as tribal council secretary for the Otoe-Missouria tribe and as chief magistrate in the Pawnee Tribal Court in Oklahoma.

Charlene Avery is a Navajo Indian, a graduate of Harvard University, and a medical doctor specializing in internal medicine. She has been an activist throughout her adult life for the improvement of health care for Native Americans and other underserved groups. She sits on the governing Board of the Association of American Indian Physicians. She has received numerous awards. She is currently clinical director of the Carl T. Curtis Health Education Center for the Omaha tribe of Nebraska.

Delfi Mondragón was born and raised in a village in New Mexico. She holds a master's degree in health service (family nurse practitioner) from the School of Medicine at the University of California at Davis, a master's of public health and a doctorate of public health from the University of California at Berkeley. She has since taught in Hawaii and Arizona, in addition to lecturing and consulting in

Europe and Latin America. She is an associate professor at the Center for Health Policy and Ethics.

This book is not meant to be all inclusive. Every speaker at the workshop emphasized the importance of asking the individual patient what they desired at a time of critical illness or near death. They also emphasized the need to approach a local group of that particular faith. They told us that these groups would be found in most major cities. The Native Americans explained that most major cities have an urban Indian center that could direct the questioner to the appropriate tribal teacher for a specific patient's needs, even if the metropolitan area does not have large numbers or a reservation in the area.

We assume that pastoral care and health care providers are familiar with the values for Christian, Catholic, or Protestant denominations. The only Christian groups included, because of their difference, are the Jehovah's Witnesses, Southwest U.S. Hispanics—mainly Catholic—and the Seventh-Day Adventists.

Several critical themes have emerged. The most striking is the similarity among the various religious groups in their acceptance of suffering in order to grow. Some expected the growth to be spiritual, some mental, and some even physical—that the patient might improve. This is important because many health care providers need to deal with acceptance of pain, suffering, and death by patients. It is also critical because of issues of not beginning or of discontinuing measures that cannot benefit the patient. Hospital ethics committees continue to deal with these issues, though less frequently.

The second critical sense that surfaced and was commented on by many is the attentiveness to each presenter and the respect demonstrated by the members of each faith toward the others. We can say that these speakers held us in rapt attention throughout the day. The environment in the room was that of teaching and learning in humbleness toward a greater goal. The spirit of love among all the faiths was evident.

As editor, I have attempted to recall this ambience and, initially, to editorially change the papers as little as possible so that authors had liberty to write as much as they thought was needed, in order to tell readers how to be supportive of patients of their culture and faith. I promptly found, however, that the strength of several authors' faith was also their chapter's downfall; they wrote extensively and with great emotion, implying "the one true faith." Clearly, writing alone is a very different dynamic from sharing with spiritual leaders of other faiths. We rewrote those chapters.

Through both processes several common themes emerge. These are very important to health care workers: 1. Always ask about a patient's customs and belief; do not assume that these chapters tell you all you need to know. 2. Allow family members to remain with critically ill and dying patients. 3. Listen to and incorporate healing rituals whenever possible.

Delfi Mondragón, Editor

Ho Chunk, *Winnebago* Perspectives on Illness and Death

Rosalee Thomas

Overview on the Winnebago:

In 1634, the Ho-Chunk people first became known to the whites. The Frenchman Nicolet came upon them near Green Bay, Wisconsin. They were located among the Sauk, the Foxes, and the Menominee, all central Algonquian tribes. They were also in touch with the Iowa, the Oto, and the Missouri tribes. These four tribes show marked similarities in their cultures and their languages.

The Winnebago also have some cultural characteristics (art and material) in common with the central Algonquians. One needs to be aware that the two influences (the Iowa, Oto, and Missouri and the central Algonquians) are intermingled in the Winnebago (Ho-Chunk).

After going south from Wisconsin and through Minnesota and South Dakota, they settled among the Omaha tribe in Nebraska. By 1836, smallpox had reduced their numbers by one-fourth. They were moved to the Territory of Iowa in 1804, where they settled first in bands after ceding their land east of the Mississippi. Disease killed many and force had to be employed to retain them on the reservation. Their new reservation was on the Omaha lands in northeast Nebraska where they have remained and have had land allocated to them in severalty.

Two divisions (the Upper or Air and the Lower or Earth) make up the Winnebago social structure. The Upper (Air) division consists of four clans and the Lower (Earth) eight clans. Air clans are: Thunderbird, War People, Eagle, and Pigeon. Earth clans are: Bear, Wolf, Elk, Deer, Fish, Water Spirit, Buffalo, and Snake. The leading clans of the divisions are the Thunderbird and the Bear, both of which have definite functions.

The Winnebago reservation is located in the northern half of Thurston County and Dixon County, all in northeastern Nebraska.

The Perspective of My Faith on the Meaning of Illness and Suffering:

The Ho-Chunk people believe that mankind is made up of the physical, social, mental, and spiritual. Thus, the balance of God, self, and nature is mandatory to experience true happiness in this life and in the hereafter. Teachings given from parent/ grandparent to children are inclusive of the holistic concept that we must always keep balance. This expression is to say that life here on this earth is not easy, and nobody ever said it would be. There would be illness and death at some time in everyone's life. There is human suffering and that is part of life. It is said that death is the most difficult to endure, but as certain as we are born, we will also meet with suffering and eventually with our demise. The Ho-Chunk people believe that we are as fragile as a root that follows along the grass and water, and when trailed, at the end of the root there is a beautiful natural creation. This creation is one created by God and it is in the form of trees, plants, animals, and human beings. If the roots are stepped upon, there is pain and even a stifling effect to its growth, and even death.

Therefore, the meaning of illness and suffering from the native perspective is that it is a part of life. We are taught that we must be strong in all ways to endure and persevere. The encouragement from elder to the young is always a lifestyle of eating, resting, and living in balance because all of these are required for strength. Water is seen as holy and as a cleanser of our being, and we must not waste it.

The Value of Suffering:

The value of suffering is strength and wisdom. We are taught that God tries us as his creation and only the strong survive. The Native belief is that we can never get used to the tangible anguish and turmoil or suffering, but if we endure, we gain an increase of strength that will carry us through this life. If we are courageous in our suffering, we will be seen by the children to be strong and courageous and this will be how they will learn to accept illness and suffering. The value of the suffering is the self-sacrifice, strength, and wisdom gained for the rest of one's life and in the hereafter.

The View of the Afterlife and Its Meaning:

The afterlife is viewed as our final place of being. The Ho-Chunk people believe in reincarnation. For the most part, the afterlife known as Heaven or the Happy Hunting Grounds is our ultimate goal in this life. We are here presently in preparation for the next life, at which time we will return to the creator (God). There is a journey that we all take to travel to the hereafter. They tell us that it is a place that is beautiful, and where we never grow old, there is no pain, and where we will want to spend eternity. They (the elders) tell us we will be greeted by our loved ones who have passed on before us. They will know us by our traditional moccasins that we wear in death, our beadwork and our dress, and they are waiting for us. If we want to join them, we must follow the road precisely, as we journey to meet them. Our ultimate reward for all of our self-sacrifice on this earth is to be with the Creator (God) and our loved ones. We can only achieve this by living a clean life.

Key Terms to Use When Dealing with a Patient:

Similar to the social work term "getting one's house in order," the question that could be asked by the medical staff is, "Are you ready to go?" This means that you are asking them if they have prepared for their demise. If the person still has a need to prepare, a family member should be called immediately. Also, another Native American should be contacted in the event a family member is not available. Perhaps there is a visitor in the hospital, or maybe there is an employee who could assist in communicating with the patient on behalf of the medical staff. In every city, there is an Urban Indian Center that could also be called to assist in finding family or to help the patient.

View on Visiting the Sick:

Sharing and caring for our tribal brothers and sisters is another tradition of the Ho-Chunk people. As a guide to living in close harmony with our fellow mankind, we must provide for those who are ill and suffering. Traditionally, the family will not leave the side of the seriously ill family member until their recovery is near or their demise is inevitable. Even after one has expired, the body is never left alone until its burial.

Post-mortem Preparation:

The Ho-Chunk people do not believe in the performance of an autopsy. They feel the person suffered enough and it will do no good to complete an autopsy because it will not bring them back to life. Only when an autopsy is ordered due to a homicidal death will family ever agree to it, and even then they will sometimes refuse.

Depending on the sex of the expired, a family member of the same sex will prepare the body for burial. They will dress them and see that they have their traditional dress so they will be recognized and accepted by their relatives when they take their journey.

The passing of a family member is treated with utmost respect. From the very first communication to the family that they have lost a loved one, the support begins flowing into the survivors. People gather to be with the surviving family members, in full support of their sorrow. Money, food, flowers, and many other gifts are given to the family of the deceased to help them with the expense for the four-day and four-night wake that is to be held. It is a very therapeutic involvement by the community to the family until the funeral takes place.

The spirit of the expired is present throughout the wake and stands at the head of the coffin until morning of the fourth day. The spirit leaves between the dark of night and the light of dawn, to be forever with the creator.

To Heal the Broken Circle: An Overview of Umo^{n}ho^n Spiritual Teaching

Rudi L. Mitchell

Practitioners of 21st-century medicine have much to gain from knowledge of traditional healing of the Indigenous Peoples of the Earth. The dominance of capital-driven science through continual use of new inventions places tremendous pressures on health care systems to forgo both preventive and therapeutic practices in favor of value-added economics.

Logos as a Term Applied to Native Belief:

The essence of aboriginal healing is a world-view that incorporates the seen and unseen as an interchangeable reality. The Greek word *Logos*, whose best English translation is "living eternal," embodies the central belief perhaps shared by nearly all Native people of the North American Continent, and much of the Indigenous world. Our relationship with Nature in real time actualizes the spiritual human experience, because we are of the Earth, an eternal gift of the Creator. If we say, "In the

Beginning was the living eternal, and the living eternal was the Creator, and the living eternal was with the Creator," we have in joint Hellenic/Native thinking not only the first verse of the Gospel of John but a universal manifestation of all religious teaching, a fact not lost among theologians and philosophers.

When applied to 21st-century medical practice, an acknowledged imperfect science, Logos provides a context for the fine-tuning of capital-intensive invention that both practitioners and investors can live with, since the concept is more an integration of paradigms rather than abandonment of one for the other. The fact that these terms, and the tone of this discussion, are used at all, shows the difficulty in translation of traditional aboriginal worldviews into modern daily usage, since the professional literature routinely dismisses native healing as simple "folk remedies" that have no "living eternal" qualities suitable for consideration in either therapeutic or preventive methodologies.

So much has been lost of indigenous medical knowledge over the course of conquest and subjugation that we will never know how successful this integration of Nature and Science would have been; clearly the ability to genetically alter natural processes does not necessarily provide either an understanding of, or improvement on, the Creator's own "inventions," as it were. Nor does the oral tradition adequately convey contemporary discernment of ancestral wisdom or competence. In the face of scientific calibration, often there is good reason to discount what we think we know or comprehend of what our elders taught.

Still, our measurement of trust as indigenous people is an awareness of the totality of our experience; for this reason, a substantial minority of Native people outright reject Christian faith for more traditional belief. In our modern time it is important to remember this distinction. While discussion goes beyond the focus of this overview, in historical terms, one could argue that without the architecture of Christianity, its structure and organization, modern science would not have evolved. Even to raise this contention exemplifies the difference.

An Overview of The Umo^{n}ho^n:

For a thousand years and more the Umo^{n}ho^n have lived as a distinct, sovereign people on this continent. That we have survived intact though migration, natural adversity, tribal raids, alien disease, cultural and religious oppression, and economic exploitation is in itself a remarkable story. Our ancestral lands along the *Nish'deke*, the "Turbid Water" of the Missouri River basin, were frequented by our forebears after we had separated from a much larger gathering of indigenous people, then living in what is called today, the Ohio River valley, many, many winters ago. From that group of the Osage, as well as the Kansa, the Oto, the Ponca, and the Quapaw, the Umo^{n}Ho^n came onto their own.

As with most aboriginal peoples who migrated to another place, once settled here, we Umo^{n}Hon became adapted to our environment. We took on the ways of the *Te'* or buffalo, whereas in the Ohio valley, fish and corn were part of our staple food.

We brought from that land a sacred ritual that became the *He'thushka*, known today in its secular form as the "Pow-Wow." One of the dances performed in a sacred manner in honor of the *He'thushka* is known in our time as the Grass Dance, universally performed across the country and around the world. The melodies and harmonies of a number of songs now used in worldly competitions are drawn from those originally composed by members of our Nation for use in our sacred *He'thushka*. For this and other reasons our Nation is considered by some to be a "Father Culture," one of a number of sovereign peoples of this continent whose contributions to aboriginal life are recognized as particularly significant.

The *Hu'thuga*, or Tribal Circle, which is the focal point of our way of life, has been shown by the science of anthropology to share with the Chinese the most intricate known kinship on earth. This is noteworthy, because with the coming of the Euro-American, our way of life began to change, long before we ceded our remaining lands through treaty with the U.S. government in 1854, establishing the present federally designated reserve along the western bluffs overlooking the *Nish'deke*. Our people were then, and remain, a deeply spiritual Nation, committed to peace and friendship with all cultures. We have few adversaries, and never went to war with the United States.

This too, is significant, because our sacred teachings bind us to an acceptance of one another in relation to our *Hu'thuga*. For the Umo^{n}Ho^n, the *Hu'thuga* continues to guide our perception of our current time with the wisdom of the ages. The commingling of the I^{n}shta'cu^{n}da, or Sky, and Ho^{n}gashenu, or Earth peoples, through the intricacies of our clanship structure has relevance as a practice for our world today, as it did in ancient times.

The Value of Illness and Suffering and Visiting the Sick:

For the Umo^{n}ho^n, the key is inclusion of everyone (and everything) in this process. Our sacred teachings bind us to an acceptance of one another in relation to our *Hu'thuga*, our tribal circle, which continues to guide with the wisdom of our elders. For this reason, while we may have traditions that outline roles to be administered by individuals, it is both the public acknowledgment and private recognition of the relationship of all things to one another that allows the life force to be given opportunity to heal a unique wound or illness within a particular person or group during a specific time.

The practice of cedaring provides comfort for the patient because our prayers to Wako^{n}da are carried forth in the smoke. (Cedaring is the burning of cedar wood.)

The View on Afterlife and its Meaning:

This is best illustrated in the following prayer:

"We hear in the wind our mother's voice, she speaks to us in our dreams. We see her image in the clouds, touch her face as we drink the waters, cradle her in our arms as we walk the earth, she is here with us, in the smoke of the cedar. It is our way to be with our elders, even among those who have passed on many, many winters ago. They are our strength, they teach us to bear the burdens of our modern world with perseverance, knowing that in time, we too, will pass."

Key Issues That Nurses, Physicians, and Clergy Might Use in Dealing with a Patient and Family at Times of Acute Illness and Death:

Placement of Umo^{n}ho^n patient's head in a hospital setting may be done in any three of the four directions but the West—which is reserved for those who have journeyed to the Spirit World. This would be of interest, and a specific custom.

Or one could speak of a designated "significant other," often an elder male relation but no one in particular, who serves as family spokesperson in the handling of all immediate practical matters once life has passed on. These are all important things to know, and observe, and that is the point: *to observe.*

All Umo^{n}ho^n beliefs connect in logical order, following in continuity as does the earth, seasons, time and events. One can thus communicate to Wako^{n}da through mediators—animals and cosmic forces, both spiritual and material—individualized in the eagle, wolf, coyote, earth, water, fire, trees, thunder, rain, lightning, wind, and the sacred smoke from the pipe.

Assistance When Physicians, Nurses, Social Workers, or Hospital Clergy Need Information for Dealing with Omaha Patients If They are Acutely Ill or Dying:

In cities there is generally an urban Indian center that has people who know where Umo^{n}ho^n people can be contacted.

Buddhist Religious Perspectives on Illness and Death

Kyoki Roberts

Overview on Zen Buddhism:

Buddhism originated in India with Siddhartha Gautama in the 6th century B.C. Although his father was the ruler of the kingdom of the Shakyas, Siddhartha renounced his life of luxury and left his father's kingdom in search of a solution to the existential suffering that he experienced himself and observed in those around him. He studied with many religious teachers and submitted himself to rigorous ascetic practices but still could not find the way to be free. He renounced all traditional religions and after years of meditation was able to pass beyond the world of intellectual distinctions and opposites to reach a level of unsurpassed integration, which is called Enlightenment. After that time, he was known as Buddha, *the Awakened One.*

Buddhism is not a system of religious dogmas. Rather, it presents a way by which all can awaken to their own Buddha-nature. Buddha Shakyamuni's teaching states that the outstanding characteristic of the human situation is frustration, which arises because of our difficulty in accepting the basic fact of life that everything around us is impermanent and transitory. Our wish to divide the perceived world into fixed, individual, and separate things does not fit with the fluid and indefinable nature of reality. In manifesting enlightenment, one is freed from these false notions.

The teaching of the Buddha quickly spread from India over much of Asia. By the beginning of the Christian Era, it had developed into at least 18 schools. The Zen School was brought to China (where it was called Ch'an) from India in the 6th century A.D. and developed into five main sub-schools. By the 13th century, the first Soto Zen school, one of the main five, was established in Japan by Dogen Zenji.

Zen is characterized by a central focus on the practice of seated mediation (zazen), and the direct transmission of Dharma from teacher to disciple. Dharma refers to the absolute truth or reality (as opposed to our ideas or beliefs about truth or reality) or to the teachings of those who have awakened to this. Zen practice in itself manifests the unity and harmony of all existence and is not limited to sitting meditation but extends to all areas of daily life.

Having given this brief background in Buddhism, I will now take up the issues specific to this conference.

The Perspective of Buddhism on the Meaning of Illness and Suffering:

As stated above, we cause our suffering when we are not in accord with the basic nature of the universe, which is that everything is impermanent, and when we see ourselves as separate or distinct from everything else.

The View of Buddhism on the Value of Suffering:

So long as we have no difficulties in our life, we go along blissfully unaware of our true nature. We call this the "heavenly realm" and all of us have experienced this at some time of our life. Ultimately, we cannot escape; it is at this moment that we have the opportunity to face reality and come to some understanding of our place in the universe.

The View of Buddhism on Afterlife and Its Meaning:

If you truly see your interconnectedness to all beings, and also the impermanence of all beings, then you realize that every moment we are born anew and die. Holding this paper you can see the tree, the rain, the sun, the earth, the logger, the mill owner, the truck driver, the diesel fuel, the shopkeeper and her family. If you see clearly, you can see the whole universe in this piece of paper. Nor is the person who walked into this room the same person reading this paper now. We have changed. This unity of all beings and this moment by moment life/death is who we are. How can you speak of the separateness of life and death; a before and an after?

Key Terms and Vocabulary That Nurses, Physicians, and Clergy Might Use in Dealing with a Buddhist Patient and His/Her Family at Times of Acute Illness and Death:

Here we are now talking about individuals. Buddhism is as diverse as Christianity, and we cannot set up a standard for all Buddhists. Those persons who were raised in predominately Buddhist countries of Asia will most likely have traditions associated more with the society they grew up in, rather than any particularly associated with Buddhism. Buddhism, and the culture it resides in, are intimately connected. As for those people who have taken up practicing Buddhism in this country, they will most likely be following traditions as followed in a local temple. Ask the person or their family.

Where to Call for Assistance When Physicians, Nurses, Social Workers, or Hospital Clergy Need Information About Dealing with Buddhist Patients, Particularly If Acutely Ill or Dying:

The patient (or if incapacitated, family and friends) is the best source of traditions and religious expectations. As a caretaker, never forget that we all share the human condition. You cannot go wrong by holding a hand, expressing your own doubts and concerns, and just being present. There is no greater gift. If you still have questions our center is available to discuss issues that might arise.

(Nebraska Zen Center, 402-551-9035). Most large cities have a Buddhist Center, listed in the telephone book under "Churches," or "Religious Organizations."

The View of Buddhism on Visiting the Sick:
The sick and dying have much to teach us of the transitory nature of our life.   Seeing our interconnectedness to all beings, compassion naturally arises.

Buddhism's Practice Regarding the Postmortem Preparation of the Body If Death Occurs:
Organ donation is a matter of individual choice. Normally a deathbed ceremony is done immediately upon death. The priest will usually ask if anyone would like to address the person who has died. As consciousness does not leave the body for three days, caretakers and family are encouraged to say anything they might not have had an opportunity to say to the deceased prior to death.

A coffin is ordered for the body. The body is washed and prepared with herbs and flowers, then dressed. The body is then taken to the family home, where an altar has been set up with pictures and mementos. Family and friends will sit with the body continually for three days. Even though people are saddened by this person's death, their state of mind is to encourage the consciousness of this person to leave the body behind and move on.

After three days a leaving-home ceremony is performed. The body is normally cremated, but

family traditions may differ.   There is another
ceremony at the crematorium.

Forty-nine days after the date of death, rebirth is
said to occur. During this time the family might
offer food every morning and perform a simple
service.   On the forty-ninth day a funeral is
performed. Again people are invited to speak to the
deceased. Often the family holds a yearly memorial
service.

The Islamic Perspective

Naeem Muhammad

The Meaning of Illness and Suffering and Its Value:

The meaning of suffering in Al-Islam is to teach humanity the higher moral and spiritual lessons from which it can grasp the deeper virtues of patience and humility, gratitude and kindness to others. The constant gravitation between the forces of good and evil is the struggle of life. In this struggle of good and evil, there is suffering and humanity is instructed with patient perseverance; this is commanded in the Quran (2:153). In Islam, suffering is looked upon as a test upon mankind, Quran (2:155). Also Allah states in the Quran for us to be firm and patient in our sufferings (2:177), to reach the soul's attainment in virtue, patient for the dignity of the soul. Three sets of circumstances are specially mentioned for the exercise of this virtue:

1. Bodily pain or suffering,
2. Adversities or injuries of all kinds, deserved and undeserved,
3. All periods of public panic, such as wars, violence, pestilence, etc.

Suffering instills the understanding and need for a compassionate human being and a caring soul; all this can lead humanity to a more peaceful life.

Illness in Islam is looked upon as one's own doing, either as a result of neglect or disobedience. In either case, the effects are the same. The Quran speaks of one wronging one's own soul, and one must purge himself of iniquities and obtain felicity by adhering to the righteous tendencies embedded in oneself. This will lead one to a *healthier life*.

On Visiting the Sick:

Islam stresses great importance on visiting the sick; it is a blessing for the one who is sick as well as for the one who is visiting the sick. For it teaches one humility and the other compassion, of which both are great virtues. Prayers should be offered for the sick.

In Islam, the one principle that is the underlying factor in humanity, to help attain the highest degree of moral and spiritual perfection, is prayer. Prayer is also the means of leveling all differences of rank, color, and nationality and the means of bringing about a cohesion and unity among humanity, which is the necessary basis of a living civilization.

Postmortem Preparation and Afterlife:

When it becomes obvious to a Muslim that he is dying, it is recommended that he turn himself in the direction of the Kabah (Qiblah). If it becomes obvious to others, who are in his presence, that death is near, and if he is unable to turn himself toward the Kabah, those present should turn him in that direction. This can be done by placing the dying person on his right side with his face and toes in the direction of the Kabah. The dying person should then be encouraged to recite the Kalimah ("There is no deity except Allah") so that these words will be the last words. Those who are present are to do this by softly repeating the Kalimah. However, the dying person should not be compelled to say the Kalimah if its recitation has a disquieting effect.

The dying person's family members, friends, and neighbors should be contacted so they may be present to help, and to encourage the Muslim in the spirit of the faith. Many prayers should be offered, and reading from the Holy Quran should be recited, especially Chapter 36 Yasin and Chapter 67 Dominion. These recitations must be offered softly so that the dying person is not disturbed. Immediately after the person dies, the big toe is to be pulled while closing the eyes, at the same time a prayer is made.

After the eyes are closed, the jaws are bound so as not to sag, and an iron object, no more than two inches in diameter, is placed upon the abdomen to keep it from becoming inflated. If possible, all the deceased person's joints should be loosened by moving them occasionally to keep the body from becoming stiff. This will facilitate its washing and shrouding.

It is forbidden in Al-Islam to break any part of the body of the deceased or to open the stomach. Prophet Muhammad (PBUH) said, "Breaking the bone of the dead is like breaking the bone of the living."

It is also forbidden to embalm the body, unless this procedure is required by the laws of one's country.

Note: It should be noted that Jewish funeral homes do not use the embalming process.

It is hated (Makruh) to put the body in a freezer because the liquids in the body expand when they are frozen, damaging the bones and internal organs.

Muslims are instructed to bury their deceased as soon as possible, before the body begins to decompose. The Prophet Muhammad, (PBUH) said, "Honor the deceased person by hurrying to bury him."

Washing the Deceased:

- A secluded, private place.
- If male, done by the closest male Muslim relative or the Imam.
- If female, done by the closest female Muslim relative.
- If no Muslim relative, then it is the duty of other Muslims or the Imam.
- There is no need to wash or pray over a stillborn infant.
- Private parts should be covered during washing.
- The water used should be lukewarm, pure, colorless, and odorless.
- A cleaning agent such as soap should be

used to cleanse the body before it is rinsed with pure water.

- In the final washing, a nonalcoholic perfume is to be added to the water.
- Before washing the deceased, the washer must make his intention.
- The washer's left hand must be covered or wrapped with a nontransparent material before washing the deceased, and it should be used when removing any unclean matter from the body.
- Cotton is placed in the openings of the ears, nose, and anus of the deceased after all unclean matter is removed.
- The washer, using the left hand beneath the sheet which covers the area from the naval to the knees, washes the private parts first then the rest of the body starting with the right side.
- Washing the body at least once is obligatory; however, the body should be washed three times or an odd number of times, up to seven.
- If impurities come out of the body during washing, the procedure must be repeated until all impurities have been expelled.
- After absolution, the hair of the head is thoroughly washed with soap.
- Next, the body is turned on its left side and washed from the neck to the foot, in front first, then in back. Then it is turned on its right side and washed in the same manner.

- After washing, the hair and body are rinsed. After final rinse, the entire body is dried with a clean towel.
- The hair should be combed and brushed. A woman's hair is to be braided into three braids if hair is long.
- A man's hair and beard should be well groomed.
- The nails are not to be cut, nor is the hair under armpits to be removed.
- Both male and female are to be groomed humbly without the use of cosmetics.
- After the above has been completed, the body is shrouded for burial.
- Cotton garments are to be used in shrouding. A loose, sleeveless, collarless shirt which covers the body from the neck to the feet for males (two sheets). A loose, sleeveless dress, which covers the body from the neck to the feet and three sheets.
- The two sheets for men are called:
    1. lower garment
    2. the winding sheet

  (It is 2 feet longer and 2 feet wider from the deceased after wrapping.)
- The three sheets for the women are called:
    1. lower garment
    2. breast wrapper or bodice
    3. the winding sheet

  (It is at least 2 feet longer and 2 feet wider than the deceased after wrapping.)
- A wrapper which will completely cover the

head and face, or a hood without a face opening, is also prescribed.

After the body has been washed, scented, and wrapped, it is placed in a coffin or bier (Mahmal) and carried to the place of prayer.

A faith in a life after death is the last of the basic principles of Islam. Death, according to the Quran, is not the end of man's life; it only opens the door to another, higher form of life! The Hereafter is not a mystery beyond the grave; it begins in this life. For the good, the heavenly life, and for the wicked, a life in hell, begin even here, though the limitations of this life do not allow most people to realize this. The Holy Quran states: "Thou wast indeed heedless of this, but now we have removed from thee thy veil, so thy sight is sharp this Day" (50122). This shows that the spiritual life which is hidden from the human eye, by reason of material limitation, will become manifest in the resurrection; because human perception will then be clearer, the veil of material limitation having been removed. There are three states in the spiritual experience of the soul. Thus the three states, death, the grave, and resurrection. This is stated this way: "Then He causes him to die, then assigns to him a grave; then when He will, He raises him to life again" (80:21-22). Three is a significant number in understanding the spiritual development of mankind. Three stages of the physical life:

1. state of being in the earth
2. state of being in the womb
3. state of being born

Another example of physical stages is the psychological or sociological concepts, being:

1. infant—childhood
2. adolescent—teenage
3. adult—adulthood

But we will stay strictly with the first physical stage.

The Quran states it this way: "And certainly we create man of an extract of clay; then we make him a small life—germ in a firm resting—placed . . . , then we cause it to grow into another creation, so blessed be Allah, The Best of Creators!" (23: 12–14)

Corresponding to these three stages in the physical development of man—the stage of dust, the stage of embryo, and the stage of birth into life—the Quran speaks of three stages in his spiritual development. The first is the growth of a spiritual life which begins in this very life, but it is a stage at which ordinarily there is no consciousness of this life, like the dust stage in the physical development of man. Then there comes death, and with it is entered the second stage of the higher or spiritual life, corresponding to the embryo stage in the physical development of man, [death = womb]. At this stage, life has taken a definite form, and a certain consciousness of that life has grown up but it is not yet the full consciousness of the final development, which takes place with the resurrection, and which may therefore be compared to the actual birth of man, to his setting forth on the road to real advancement, to a full awakening of the great truth.

The development of the higher life in the grave is as necessary a stage in the spiritual world as is the development of physical life in the embryonic state. The two thus stand on a par. An inner self that assumes a shape after death and forms the first spiritual body in the grave and is then developed into the body in resurrection. The afterlife is the goal, final, and completion of the soul's journey through the process of what we understand to be life.

Key Terms and Vocabulary:
1. Allah: Deity, one who is worshiped, the creator.
2. As-salaam-Alaikam: Peace be upon you.
3. Wa-Alaikum-As-Salaam: Peace be returned onto you.
4. Al-Quran: Holy Book
5. Imam: A spiritual leader
6. Al-Fatiha: Opening chapter of Al-Quran
7. Al-Salat: Prayer
8. Dua: Short prayers
9. Sura: Chapter
10. Ayat: Verse
11. Kalimal: Words of oath
12. Janazah: Funeral

Where to Call for Assistance When Physicians, Nurses, Social Workers, or Hospital Clergy Need Information About Dealing with Muslim Patients, Particularly If Acutely Ill or Dying:
The patient or family and friends are the best source of this information. If you have further

questions, most large cities have an Islamic Center, listed in the telephone book under "Mosques," "Churches," or "Religious Organizations."

In Nebraska or the surrounding rural areas:
Massid Dar-Al-Islam
4426 Florence Blvd.
Omaha, NE 68102

Contact: Imam Naeem T. A. Muhammad
at Residence: (402) 551-6134
at Work: (402) 451-7766, or
Islamic Center of Omaha
3511 North 73rd St.
Omaha, NE 68134
(402) 571-0720

In the name of Allah the Beneficent, the Merciful
The Perspective of the Nation of Islam

Melvin Muhammad

An Overview of the Nation of Islam:

The Nation of Islam was founded July 1930 by Mr. W. F. Muhammad. Mr. Muhammad came to Detroit, Michigan, and began selling silk material, door to door, to the residents in what was termed, "Black Bottom." This was an area in Detroit that was economically, politically, and spiritually depressed. The inhabitants of this section of the community were black.

While selling these materials Mr. Muhammad would occasionally be invited into the homes of the people. Once inside, Mr. Muhammad would discuss with the people the religion of their brothers and sisters in the East. Hearing this new teaching, the message of "Islam," the people wanted to know more. Mr. Muhammad asked that they invite their friends and neighbors, and upon his return that evening, he would share this message. Thus began the international organization known today as the "Nation of Islam." The Nation of Islam is now and has always been a spiritual movement, fighting for freedom, justice, and equality for all people.

Mr. W. F. Muhammad met with and taught one Elijah Poole, later known as Elijah Muhammad, for three and a half years, the wisdom and knowledge of the universe and the essence of creation. Mr. W. F. Muhammad commissioned Elijah Muhammad to continue the work among the black men and women of north America, for the scriptures foretold of a people in the last days, that would be blind, deaf, and dumb to the knowledge of God, self, and their open enemy. Elijah, upon the departure of his teacher W. F. Muhammad, announced to Detroit and the world that he had met with and had been taught by God in the person of W. F. Muhammad. The honorable Elijah Muhammad taught this message for forty-four years while he was physically among his people, and Minister Louis Farrakhan continues to teach this message of self-sufficiency under the guidance of the honorable Elijah Muhammad. These three men have been and continue to be the most successful men in teaching self-independence among the masses of black people.

The Meaning of Illness and Suffering and Its Value:

The meaning of illness and suffering one experiences in their life has many implications. Often illness is brought about by improper dietary practices. In the Nation of Islam, Muslims are instructed to eat one meal a day; this is practiced as best one can. There are always exceptions to any school of thought or training. Women who are pregnant or nursing their children can eat one meal per day; however, it is best that they practice eating at least two meals per day. Muslims in the Nation of Islam who practice these dietary restrictions have very few illnesses; if illness does occur it does not last very long. This practice is quite simple and is as follows:

A. We understand from the teachings of the most honorable Elijah Muhammad that food is the substainer of life, and food also has the ability to destroy life. Today's food chain is so full of pesticide, chemicals, insecticides, and animal growth hormones that the body unfortunately begins to store these agents of death.

B. By eating one meal every 24 hours, the Muslim in the Nation of Islam allows the body to properly digest the food. We understand that it takes at least 8 hours for the stomach to properly digest the food.

The Value of Suffering:

Suffering is looked upon as a necessary part of spiritual growth, and physical suffering can be beneficial. However, in this world of good and evil we understand that suffering can sometimes be viewed as struggle. Struggle is ordained by Allah, and Allah is a merciful god. Suffering is prescribed by Allah, for man and woman. Through suffering one struggles just as all things in existence struggle to come forth into existence. Suffering is likened to this type of struggle.

The value in suffering is a part of life and is a fact of death. One must never run from suffering simply because Allah is he that is in control of all things. There is nothing independent of Allah, and all things depend on Allah. When one suffers, one should gain understanding that everything has an effect. Where there is an effect, there is always a cause. Man must search his soul and mind to uncover the reality of his/her suffering. What is the cause?

Through prayer we may not find the answers that we seek; however, there is no prayer that goes unanswered. We must never direct prayer for material gain. Prayer should be for forgiveness and spiritual enlightenment. Sincere prayer is always answered. We often fail to understand how, when, and in what form our prayer is answered.

Postmortem Preparation and View of Afterlife:

All Muslims, regardless of their school of faith or teachings, practice the same preparation procedures. Due to brevity, I will respond to this inquiry.

Muslims in the Nation of Islam do not prescribe to a belief in life after death. At least not a physical life after death. If the body comes from the earth and to the earth it shall return, the questions that are raised are many. We believe that once you spiritually die, soon physical death overtakes you. The belief of life after death is very simple. Man is currently on a dead lever mentally, economically, religiously, socially, morally, as well as spiritually. For the Muslims in the Nation of Islam, the honorable Elijah Muhammad teaches that there is no such thing as life after a physical death. Matter is neither created nor destroyed. It has always existed just as electricity has always existed. The human body is only an illusion of what can be seen by the outer eye. The essence of who one is cannot be seen by the outer eye; it must be viewed by the inner eye, the breath of life (soul) of the individual.

We believe that heaven and hell exist here on this earth. Many of the poor, disadvantaged, elderly, children, black, brown, red, yellow, and white, know no other condition of life other than hell, whereas an elite few know just the opposite (heaven on earth) while they live.

Mathematically and scientifically, physical life after physical death does not exist. Never has, nor never will on our level of understanding.

We believe life is a time continuum that exists in three stages:

A. Past (Ancestors)
B. Present (Self)
C. Future (Offspring)

Therefore one never really dies, because through one's genetic makeup, man has the ability to recreate himself over and over again.

Visiting the Sick and Elderly:
The honorable Elijah Muhammad teaches that

we all owe a debt to our elders; therefore we should honor them. Everyone has to work out their own salvation. Humanity should show compassion for the sick, elderly, and confined. We can never know the beneficial effect we have on a person who becomes ill, or is confined. This should be practiced by everyone and can lead to greater spiritual awareness. The holy Q'ran states "man gets what he strives for."

Where to Call for Assistance When Physicians, Nurses, Social Workers, or Hospital Clergy Need Information About Dealing with Nation of Islam Patients, Particularly If Acutely Ill or Dying:

The national organization headquarters in Chicago is the best source of this information, if the patient is not in a large city:

Mosque Maryam
Attn: Ishamel Muhammad, Regional Minister
7351 S. Stony Island Ave
Chicago, IL 60649
(312) 324–6000

If you have further questions, most large cities have an Islamic Center, listed in the telephone book under "Mosques," "Churches," or "Religious Organizations."

In Nebraska or the surrounding rural areas:
Minister Melvin Muhammad
2002 N. 45th St.
Omaha, NE 68104
(402) 556–7639 (Home)
(402) 455–6340 (Office)
(402) 977–3281 (Pager)

Tradition in the Modern World: Jewish Perspectives on Illness and Death

Leonard J. Greenspoon
Klutznick Chair in Jewish Civilization, Creighton University

Overview:

There is a Jewish tradition that when God gave the Torah or Hebrew Bible to humans, He also gave them the right and responsibility to interpret it. Their collective interpretation would stand even if it went against divine intention.

It appears that today's Jews, or most of us at least, have taken this tradition quite personally, for there is considerable insight in the oft-quoted saying: Ask 10 Jews for their view on something, and you'll get 10 (or 20 or more) different opinions.

All of this is, I hope, an appropriate way to introduce my presentation and what is to be one of its major themes: It is difficult, if not impossible, to generalize when dealing with Jewish attitudes toward anything—suffering, death, and the afterlife definitely included. It is very important for sensitive health care providers to understand this point, since they may well find that what is a central point of belief for one Jewish person is not at all important to another; what one Jewish family considers an indispensable religious ritual is not practiced and may even be severely criticized or seriously questioned by another.

The reason for this is that even in its most traditional forms Judaism is not a dogmatic or monolithic religion. Throughout its history Jewish leaders have generally resisted the temptation to systematize or dogmatize beliefs and practices. For this reason it is almost always an error and a mark of considerable insensitivity to brand one individual a bad Jew and extol another as a good Jew on the basis of lifestyle.

At the same time, it is recognized that through the centuries some beliefs and practices have become traditional for large numbers of Jews. As we discuss some specific questions, we will take care to point out the traditional approach (where it exists)—not because it is better or worse, but precisely because it is traditional. Historically, even those Jews who have updated the tradition or found tradition outdated have been familiar with tradition. Unfortunately, this is no longer the case, so that it may well happen that non-Jews are called upon to answer questions about Jewish tradition. That is another reason for my decision to include traditional answers, even if these are no longer directly applicable to most patients and families of patients.

Membership in a synagogue or temple (both terms refer to a Jewish "house of worship") is not as statistically high as is church membership in many Christian denominations. Many nonsynagogue (non-Temple) members nonetheless consider themselves Jewish. Painted in broad strokes, the religiouslyactive American Jewish community can be divided into three movements or branches on the basis of their attitude toward tradition.

The most traditional Jews are generally identified with Orthodox Judaism; the least traditional or the most part identify themselves with the Reform Movement. In between are Conservative Jews. Given the fact that the Orthodox lifestyle generally requires a number of specific facilities—a synagogue within walking distance, a ritual bath, kosher butchers and restaurants, and so forth—Orthodox communities are generally found only in and around larger cities. Although Omaha does not have all of these institutions in place, it nonetheless supports a vibrant, and I might add varied, Orthodox Jewish community. I add the word "varied" to emphasize the fact that within each grouping there is variety, to a greater or lesser degree. Thus, an Orthodox Jewish patient is likely to require some special foods and may well want time set aside for daily and Sabbath worship and for other religious observances. But the exact nature of the food and of these observances will differ.

Because Reform Judaism has typically placed less emphasis on the particulars of Jewish tradition, Reform Jews are somewhat less likely than others to have special requirements based on religion. Such requirements may be an issue, however, when other Jews are present as visitors. Because some (but not all or even most) Conservative Jews do maintain traditional dietary laws and related practices, their position as patients (as in other areas of life) is frequently in the middle. Since neither Reform nor Conservative Jews require the array of distinctive services common in Orthodox communities, they tend to be found in smaller as well as in larger metropolitan areas. Both are present in the Omaha area.

Visiting the Sick:

There is one other general observation with specific applicability to the topics under discussion here: the family. Traditionally, Judaism has been a family-centered religious and cultural community. In common with almost all other ethnic and religious groups, the bonds of family have suffered some loosening in recent decades. Happily, we can note that an emphasis on family is still a central feature of Judaism. With specific reference to our topic, I am able to report that the tradition of visiting the sick, whether they are family or friends, continues to this day among almost all Jews. This practice keeps alive one of the most visible ways in which Jews demonstrate their commitment through an act of kindness or charity. So important was this practice that Jewish communities regularly established Societies for Visiting the Sick, so that no Jew would ever feel alone or separated from family in his or her time of need.

So it is that "family" is to be understood in as extended a meaning as possible. We all have "aunts" and "uncles" to whom we feel very close, but with whom we share no genetic connection. They are as near and dear as any "real" relative can be. And every member of this "family" feels qualified to offer an opinion on just about every topic. Going back to the story I related at the beginning of this presentation, we may even be bold enough to say that such "opinionatedness" is a God-given right.

Illness and Suffering:

Serious illness with its accompanying suffering is in Judaism, as in other Western monotheistic faiths, at one and the same time a simple and a complex matter. Simple: Serious illness may be viewed as a deserved punishment for the accumulation of sins committed by a particular person. An individual who is cured is to interpret his/her illness as a call for repentance and atonement. Those for whom a serious illness turns into a fatal one can be judged as guilty of even greater wrongs and/or as squanderers of earlier opportunities for repentance. A just God would surely not inflict suffering except on those deserving of it. As the Hebrew Bible or Old Testament makes clear, the reward for good deeds is more to be found in the quality of life than in its quantity. So those who suffer much, including the pain of illness, must have sinned much.

Even in the Hebrew Bible, however, this simple

view is called into question. Look at the book of Job. Here a righteous (though certainly not perfect) man suffers the most painful physical and mental afflictions we can imagine. Although his so-called friends urge him to consider his supposedly sinful ways and to repent, Job knows—as do we as readers—that his terrible punishments far exceed what he deserves. We are led to raise some troubling questions: Is God really not all that good (the question of theodicy or divine justice)? Could He be guilty of "cruel and unusual punishment"? Or is it the case that there are forces of evil, leading to human suffering, that are beyond His control (the issue of omnipotence)? The author of the book of Job does not offer any easy answers to such queries. Rather, the finite Job is challenged to defend his questioning of God's infinite power. Along with Job, we have to admit that we cannot totally comprehend the ways of God.

Special Prayers:

Traditional Judaism is heir to both the simpler and the more complex view of serious illness and the suffering that accompanies it. This ambiguity comes to the fore especially when we feel that a loved one has died in a particularly tragic way, as a result of a senseless accident, or before his/her time. It is human to be angry, to question, to wonder; it is the bedrock of faith that keeps us going. Such faith is especially visible in a remarkable Jewish prayer called the Kaddish or sanctification. Although this prayer is part of every service, it has a special role as the Mourner's Prayer. Even as we question God, we affirm His constancy, His justice, His care for the created world. As we sanctify God, we reaffirm our faith.

And it is also worthy of note—to return to our earlier theme of family and community—that the Kaddish is one of the few Jewish prayers that we cannot say alone. In traditional Judaism 10 adult males make up the minimum number of a "congregation" in the midst of which we may recite the Kaddish. In other forms of Judaism the number 10 is generally preserved, but the adults can be either males or females. In all cases, the questioning that is natural in such crises is channeled into a statement of faith, and this is shared with members of our family and community. This is also the case with prayers for the sick that are recited either at the hospital or in the synagogue.

While such beliefs and practices are widespread, more secular Jews may dispense entirely with any idea that God has a direct connection with illness. For such individuals, more scientific or medical explanations suffice. In this situation, as in so many others, the medical professional must remain sensitive to such differences and must never challenge a patient with the charge that he/she has not followed traditional Jewish belief or practice.

For almost all Christians the question of suffering is tightly linked to firm beliefs about the afterlife, to which the resurrected go for reward and punishment. It is interesting to observe that explicit affirmations about such concepts are largely absent from the Hebrew Bible, whose writers have a decidedly this-worldly outlook. In this instance, as in others, it is equally important to note that traditional Judaism is not always equivalent to Biblical Israel. In the centuries around the time of Jesus most Jews came to believe in an afterlife with reward and punishment and in the concept of resurrection. (Thus, although Jews do not accept Jesus as the Messiah, the divine son of God, nonetheless there is nothing remarkable—from the traditional Jewish point of view—in affirming that he was resurrected.) These very beliefs find expression in central prayers that are part of the liturgy of all branches of modern Judaism. Although a Reform Jew may understand such language in a different way from an Orthodox Jew, this is compelling evidence of the retention of traditional concepts.

Afterlife:

For many Jews, the fate of the individual is in some way connected with the ultimate end of the whole created order, when the Messiah comes to destroy the wickedness of the world and judge its inhabitants. Again, this is taken quite literally by many Orthodox Jews, while others speak more generally of a future age when humans through their own energies are able to create a better world for all. There is likewise diversity of opinion, even among traditional Jews, over whether "heaven" is a specific location or something more akin to a state of being.

It is then not easy to formulate one's response to

questions about suffering, the afterlife, etc., in Judaism or among Jews. Certainly the more traditional explanations urge us to find comfort in even seemingly undeserved suffering as we affirm in the present our belief in God and look forward in the future to an ultimate vindication in the afterlife. Such a formulation is not meaningful to less traditional Jews, many of whom do not hold to a belief in the afterlife in spite of the wording they may find in their prayer books. Through their own experience, it may be assumed, they have found some resolution to the lack of fairness and equity that characterizes life, especially during times of crisis. It would be worthwhile for health care practitioners to encourage patients to vocalize their faiths, as well as their frustrations, whenever time allows.

Key Terms:

Given the variety of beliefs and practices we have already observed (and there is more to come), it is easy to see that individual Jews may very well use very different vocabulary to express their feelings and that at the same time some individuals will use very similar terms with diverse significances. As if that were not enough, we hasten to add that even relatively secular Jews may use a Hebrew or Yiddish (largely a combination of Hebrew and German) expression rather than the English equivalent. The same is true to an even greater extent among the many family and community members who pay frequent visits to the sick. In spite of these inherent difficulties, I have provided a glossary of key terms. While I have made every effort to formulate the definitions as inclusively as possible, I would continue to urge medical professionals to keep their ears, their eyes, and their minds open and, whenever in doubt, to ask.

The admonition to seek additional information and/or clarification through asking naturally extends beyond the patient and his/her family. Every Jewish community, even a small one, has a network of institutions and individuals to provide services, aid, and comfort during difficult times. For the Omaha-area Jewish community, I am appending a few names and numbers that will be useful. I have no doubt that these individuals and agencies will be more than willing and able to provide further guidance. I say this especially because the Omaha Jewish community, of about 7,000, is famous worldwide for its generosity and activities on behalf of Jewish causes. And since, as they say, charity begins at home, we can expect to find exemplary resources here.

If Death Occurs:

We have already had occasion to observe that visiting the sick is a central act of kindness among all Jews. This community-centered principle does not stop here, however. If an illness is fatal and the patient dies, traditional Jewish practice is to have someone stay with the body from the moment of death to the time of burial. Where family members are not available or are otherwise occupied in preparing for the funeral, volunteers from the community take turns sitting by the body and offering prayers.

Postmortem Care:

There are also traditional practices associated with preparation of the body for burial. Again, the community emphasis comes to the fore. Even in the relatively small Jewish community of Greenville, SC, where I lived for many years before coming to Omaha, there was a group ready to prepare the body and a local mortuary that made this possible by providing appropriate facilities. Water is poured over the body to the accompaniment of prayers, and the body is then carefully, we might even say lovingly, washed. In keeping with a sense of dignity, only females prepare the body of a dead woman; males, for deceased men. This sense of propriety extends to making sure that high standards of decency and decorum are adhered to throughout the process. The dead body is not identical to the living person, but it is fully deserving of respect.

Following the bathing of the body, males are clothed in a simple white garment, and both males and females are buried in plain wooden coffins (usually of pine). These practices are to remind us that we should all leave this world as we came into it—equally. Reform and some Conservative Jews follow different practices, but seek to maintain the same high standards of dignity and equality.

It is not surprising, things being what they are these days, that some people choose to follow a more ostentatious approach in death as they did in life. I am tempted to abandon my neutrality at this point, but will content myself with the simple statement that all such showiness is not just untraditional, it is antitraditional.

There are serious debates within the Jewish community concerning if and when to remove life support systems, and I am not able on this occasion to deal with the series of ethical and legal issues such debate entails. I should mention, if only briefly, that traditionally Jews have resisted autopsies as an infringement on the dignity due even to a dead person. Reform Jews are somewhat more lenient. All branches of Judaism will accede to a legal request for autopsies, however. In the area of organ transplants the highest principle of "reverence for life" frequently (but not always) takes precedence over all others. In this instance, the result is often approval of organ transplants that result in the maintenance of life for another (as in a heart transplant) or in the substantial improvement of another's quality of life (as in cornea transplants). But there are no universals even here.

Given the multiplicity of beliefs and practices prevalent among Jews today and the nervousness that naturally attends any serious or fatal illness, it is not inconceivable that medical professionals may find themselves in the role of umpires if an argument unfortunately develops among family or friends. Remaining sensitive to the situation and seeking expert advice are naturally the ways to approach this difficult circumstance.

Burial:

I think it would be useful for me to say a few words about burial and mourning practices among Jews, especially because we see operative in them the same principles that are visible while the individual was alive.   Burial ceremonies are typically simple occasions, with members of family and community in attendance. Community members make it a practice to visit and to bring food to the homes of mourners and to assure that they are as comfortable in all ways as possible. As mentioned above, friends gather daily to make up the congregation necessary for recitation of the mourners' Kaddish.

Continuing Ritual in Mourning:

I like to think that we can detect considerable psychological and sociological insight on the part of those who initiated and developed Jewish practices in the areas we have been considering. The same is true when we come to grieving and mourning. At first, it seemed strange to me that an effort was made to institutionalize or regulate such a personal matter as grieving. But, upon further reflection, the Jewish approach seems to make eminent good sense. It is inappropriate to grieve too little, as it were to appear to forget the deceased; it is equally inappropriate to grieve too much, as it were to remain in the past and not get on with one's life. So Jewish tradition formulates a short period of seven days for intense grieving, and then a longer period of months for the gradual reentry of mourners into everyday life. The anniversary of the deceased's death is observed each

year, so that the memory will stay alive.   The
Kaddish is also recited on these occasions.

In my presentation I have sought to do two
things: one more general and one at the level of
specifics. I do not think that a list of do's and don'ts
is very meaningful unless the context for such
practices is established. This I have attempted to do
by speaking of certain traditional Jewish principles.
The application of these principles among modern
Jews is quite varied, given varying attitudes toward
Jewish tradition.   Nonetheless, concepts such as
family, dignity, and propriety are equally important
for observant and secular Jews.   I have urged
professionals to be sensitive both to the common
features of Jewish belief and practice and to the
infinite variations and permutations that can be
observed among real patients on an everyday basis.
Although it is clear that the primary duty of doctors,
nurses, and others is to offer the very highest level
of care, they might—as time permits—listen and
learn about a religion and culture that is apart from
theirs but part of the society that makes up this city,
this region, and this nation.

Fifteen Key Terms in Judaism:

Chevra kadddisha: In Hebrew this phrase literally
means "holy brotherhood or society." It refers to a
group of Jewish individuals who volunteer to look
after the needs of the dying and the requirements of
the dead.

Kaddish: This prayer of praise to God (whose title
literally means "sanctification" in the Aramaic

language) is part of every Jewish service. It is recited by those in mourning provided that a minyan is present (see below).

Kashrut: This Hebrew word comes from the root meaning "fit or proper." It refers to the dietary laws through which observant Jews prepare and eat their food. A related word is "kosher."

Kevod ha-mayt: This Hebrew phrase means "the honor that is owed to the deceased person."

Minyan: This Hebrew term refers to the minimum quorum or number (in Hebrew the word means "number") of 10 adults who constitute a congregation, in the midst of which certain prayers such as the Kaddish (see above) may be recited. Traditionally, the 10 adults must be males; women are counted "in the minyan" among less traditional Jews today.

Nichoom avayleem: This Hebrew phrase refers to "consoling or comforting the mourners."

Olam ha-ba: This Hebrew phrase literally means "the world to come." It may be used in discussing Jewish concepts of the afterlife.

Pikkuach nefesh: This Hebrew phrase may be translated as "reverence or consideration for human life." In practice, this principle means that any ritual command may be set aside when human life or health is endangered.

Sheloshim: The less intense mourning period of 30 days (in Hebrew, sheloshim literally means "thirty") that follows the funeral. See also shiva (below).

Shiva: The seven-day period (in Hebrew, shiva literally means "seven") after the funeral set aside for the most intense mourning. We generally speak of "sitting" shiva.

Taharah: This Hebrew word comes from the root meaning "to purify" and refers to the traditional way of ritually washing the body and wrapping it in a simple white shroud.

Tzedakah: This Hebrew word comes from the root meaning "righteous." In general, it refers to charitable giving. Traditionally in Judaism there has been a close connection between "giving" tzedakah and honoring the memory of a loved one.

Yahrzeit: This Yiddish expression (see below) refers to the anniversary of the death of a close relative. The date of Yahrzeit is traditionally calculated in accordance with the Hebrew calendar.

Yiddish: This refers to a language that combines Hebrew words and expressions with German and to a lesser extent with several others. Although few American Jews know the language well, most are familiar with a few of the more colorful and expressive words and phrases.

Yizkor: This Hebrew word comes from the root meaning "to remember" and refers to the memorial service held four times a year in most traditional Jewish communities.

Select Annotated Bibliography:

Goodman, Arnold M. *A Plain Pine Box: A Return to Simple Jewish Funerals and Eternal Traditions.* New York: KTAV. The subtitle of this volume clearly indicates its thrust.

Grollman, Earl A. *Concerning Death: A Practical Guide for the Living.* Boston: Beacon Press. A practical anthology by experts that includes a chapter on Judaism.

Klein, Isaac. *A Guide to Jewish Religious Practice.* New York: The Jewish Theological Seminary of America.   This volume, written from the perspective of Conservative Judaism, covers a large number of issues, including those related to sickness and death.

Lamm, Maurice. *The Jewish Way in Death and Mourning.* New York: Jonathan David. Although written from the Orthodox or traditional point of view, this valuable book is the standard reference for anyone interested in these topics.

Maslin, Simeon. *Gates of Mitzvah.* Cincinnati: Central Conference of American Rabbis. This volume, written by experts in the Reform movement, includes a full discussion of practices relating to death and dying.

Riemer, Jack. *Jewish Reflections on Death.* New York: Schocken. This is a strong collection of essays that look at all aspects of death.

Select Resources within the Omaha Jewish Community:
Synagogues [Note: You will want to avoid calling synagogues, especially Orthodox ones, on the

Sabbath and on Jewish holidays. In Judaism the "day" begins at sunset and lasts until the next sunset. So, for example, the Sabbath begins at sunset on Friday and continues to Saturday sunset. As a result, the Jewish "day" begins and ends quite early in mid-winter, quite late during the summer.]

Temple Israel (402-556-6536): The Reform congregation of Omaha.

Chabad House (402-697-1124): The Lubavitcher Chasidic congregation of Omaha. (Chasidic Jews are members of an Orthodox community that maintains distinctive codes of dress, diet, and ritual, in addition to adhering to the Tradition.)

Beth-El Synagogue (402-492-8550): The Conservative congregation of Omaha.

B'nai Israel (402-322-4705): A Reconstructionist congregation in Council Bluffs. Reconstructionism is a small but growing movement that views Judaism as an evolving religious civilization.

Beyt Shalom (402-291-3469): A Reconstructionist congregation in Omaha.

Beth Israel Synagogue (402-556-6288): The Orthodox congregation of Omaha.

Community-wide Organizations [Whenever possible, you will want to follow the practice outlined above to contact these agencies.]

Bureau for the Aging: The key person to contact is Shane Kotok, CSW, MS (402-334-6529), who is Director of Social Services.

Jewish Family Service: The main number is 402-330-2024.

Jewish Federation: The main number is 402-334-8200.

Where to Call for Assistance When Physicians, Nurses, Social Workers, or Hospital Clergy Need Information About Dealing with Jewish Patients, Particularly If Acutely Ill or Dying:
The patient's family and friends are the best source of traditions and religious expectations. Most large cities have a **Synagogue** listed in the telephone book under "Churches," "Temples," or Religious Organizations."

The Perspective of Jehovah's Witnesses

Ronald Rieckman

Overview of Jehovah's Witnesses:

J ehovah's Witnesses are a Christian society. They base their beliefs and morals on the Bible. They believe the earth is to be restored to a paradise condition by means of God's Kingdom. Jesus Christ is their model for daily life and is recognized as their Savior. They refer to Almighty God as Jehovah and therefore call themselves Jehovah's Witnesses. They feel that the faithful Bible prophets of old constituted a long line of Jehovah's Witnesses.

In modern times Jehovah's Witnesses were organized under the legal organization of Zion's Watch Tower Tract Society in 1884. This was a nonprofit corporation with headquarters located at Allegheny, Pennsylvania. Charles Taze Russell was selected as president. A few years later this corporation's name was changed to the Watch Tower Bible and Tract Society of Pennsylvania. In due time an additional nonprofit corporation, the

Watchtower Bible and Tract Society of New York, Inc., was formed. In 1909 the headquarters was moved to the Columbia Height area of Brooklyn, New York, where it is presently located. Their chief publication is the *Watchtower* magazine. The first edition was published in 1879. In 1996 the *Watchtower* was published in 125 languages with an average printing of 18 million copies of each issue. Jehovah's Witnesses are an international organization with over five million members in over 230 lands.

The first president, Charles Taze Russell served until his death in 1916 and then was replaced by Joseph F. Rutherford. In 1942 Nathan H. Knorr became president; he introduced a period of intensive training in the organization. He began several congregation schools, including a missionary training school, the Watchtower Bible School of Gilead. The current president is Milton G. Henschel.

The Perspective of Jehovah's Witnesses on the Meaning of Illness and Suffering:

We do not believe that we are predestined to experience a certain illness, as though God wanted us to have a certain illness. Illness, we feel, can arise due to a number of different reasons. It could be poor diet, living a high, risk lifestyle, or exposure to a contagious disease. Hereditary factors can predispose a person to a certain disease. Although there are a few rare instances of divine curses in the Holy writings, we do not feel that at this time God directly causes illness to persons, such as that God has cursed certain persons with AIDS. However as a result of not adhering to God's moral laws, AIDS may come about.

Although there are a few references to divine healing in the Holy Bible, we also do not feel that at this time there is divine healing. Even the Bible talks about one of the disciples being sick and being encouraged to follow a course of medication; it also refers to another disciple as being a physician. We appreciate what the medical community does in our behalf and we go to hospitals for health care. We do not believe it was part of God's purpose for mankind to experience illness and suffering and we feel that in the future millennium illness and death will be eliminated by the restoration of the earth to a paradise.

The Perspective of Jehovah's Witnesses on the Value of Suffering:

We do not believe that God causes pain and suffering. If a person suffers due to an illness, we feel it is very unfortunate. At times when a person may suffer from some sort of disease, it can be very discouraging and depressing. A person may have very little control over what is happening. At times like this a person needs inner strength and fortitude. If a person survives this ordeal it can strengthen their faith and produce a stronger person.

The Perspective of Jehovah's Witnesses on the Afterlife and Its Meaning:

We believe in what the Holy writings call the resurrection, that God can restore a person to life, either to heavenly life or to life in the restored paradise earth, in the future. We do not believe that a person experiences any distress or agony after death. At the time of death a person ceases all consciousness; there are no thoughts, no pain, no anxiety. We believe death is the opposite of life. We are convinced a person is a soul and when he/she dies the soul dies. We do not believe there is any torture or discomfort after death. When a person dies he/she waits for a resurrection if God extends it to that person.

Key Terms and Vocabulary That Nurses, Physicians, and Clergy Might Use When Dealing with the Jehovah's Witness Patient and His Family at Times of Acute Illness and Death:
At times of serious illness or death it certainly would be of great support to be able to relate to the patient and family in terminology they feel comfortable in, and to converse on subjects that would have a positive emotional effect on them. At this juncture three key terms/subjects would be of great solace to the family:
1. Paradise
2. Resurrection
3. Prayer
As to the first one, ask about their belief in the paradise earth; this provides hope for them. Perhaps state, "Although I personally don't believe in the paradise, I know you do. Tell me about it." In the event of death the subject of the resurrection can be discussed, such as, "I know your mother was a fine person and God will surely remember her in the

resurrection." Prayer would be an appropriate subject. We believe that prayer, in addition to providing comfort and being a way of communicating with God, can also produce real results. There are other key terms and vocabulary expressions that we would be well to be acquainted with, so as to be able to converse with the patient and family and to be able to support them in their faith: We refer to our religious leaders as *elders*. Those who engage in special missionary work we refer to as *pioneers*. We affectionately refer to all of our members, regardless if they are a pioneer or elder, as *"brother"* and *"sister"* ("Brother and Sister Smith were here to see you"). We refer to our religious groups as *congregations* (the Ralston Congregation, the Dundee Congregation, etc.). We call our religious buildings *Kingdom Halls;* our local Kingdom Hall gatherings we term *meetings;* larger gatherings held three times a year we term *assemblies* or *conventions* ("How was your convention this past summer in Lincoln?"). Another key term is that we refer to God by the divine name *Jehovah,* and so we call ourselves his witnesses, that is, Jehovah's Witnesses, or we abbreviate it and call ourselves *"Witnesses."*

Where Physicians, Nurses, Social Workers, and Hospital Clergy Can Call for Assistance, When Needing Information to Deal with a "Witness" Patient:

Each hospital has a pastoral representative of ours assigned to look after *all* of Jehovah's Witnesses that come to that particular hospital for care. Their name and number are on file with the pastoral care department. If you are unable to locate that name, you may call any of the Kingdom Halls listed in the phone book. We are listed under churches, and then under Jehovah's Witnesses, ask to speak to one of the elders and he will gladly assist you, or you may ask the patient or family for the name of one of their elders.

Also in the major cities, we have Hospital Liaison Committees that deal with the special needs of our people when they want to use an alternative form, rather than blood transfusions. These Liaison committees deal with the more difficult medical cases, while the pastoral representative handles the regular visitation. Because I serve on the Omaha Hospital Liaison Committee, I can assure that we are ready and willing to assist. Usually we can be contacted through the hospital administration or you may call any one of the Kingdom Halls and ask for a Hospital Liaison member.

The View of Jehovah's Witnesses on Visiting the Sick:

We feel visiting the sick has a positive effect and can be encouraging to the patient and family. On rare occasion one of our members may not desire any visitation for some reason, or perhaps they desire visits from a very small circle of friends or relatives. This should be respected. Ordinarily, though, hospital personnel can respect and support the patient by assisting in the visitation process by notifying the pastoral representative, or by asking, "Is there anyone you would like me to call for you?"

As to the actual visit, if hospital personnel choose to visit, a person would need to be judicious, not staying too long, taking into consideration each person's particular situation, etc.   There is no particular ceremony or ritual that needs to be performed while the patient is hospitalized.   On occasion they may want to engage in private prayer, or when they receive visits from their pastoral representative, they may want to quietly share in a simple prayer for a minute or two.   They should be shown respect on these occasions, thus respecting them as one piece in this great mosaic of patients of many faiths.

The Witnesses' Practices in Postmortem Preparation of the Body:

There are no special preparations that need to be made by health care workers.   The only item of concern is the performing of an autopsy.   Although it is not expressly forbidden, many of our people may not wish for it to be done.   Obviously the family should be consulted on this, first, as is general hospital policy.   Otherwise, it is, for the most part, just a matter of inquiring which funeral parlor the family desires the body to be moved to, and then working with the family in that regard.   As to the burial itself, some of our people may choose cremation; others may opt for a "traditional" burial.

Other Special Needs of Jehovah's Witnesses When Hospitalized:

Due to Jehovah's Witnesses declining blood transfusions, they need to be understood in this area.

Some may feel they reject all medical care; others may not be sure of what they will or will not accept in regard to blood-related issues. First of all, we (Jehovah's Witnesses) come to the hospitals because we desire quality health care. *We do not accept whole blood transfusions nor the major components of blood, RBCS, WBCS, plasma, or platelets.* We generally will accept extracorporeal devices, and blood fractions, such as albumin and blood factors. Our people appreciate being supported in their convictions and any assistance in locating alternatives is appreciated.

Jehovah's Witnesses

Religious and Ethical Positions on Medical Therapy, Child Care, and Related Matters

Abortion:

Deliberately induced abortion simply to avoid the birth of an unwanted child is the willful taking of human life and hence is unacceptable to Jehovah's Witnesses. If (at the time of childbirth) a choice must be made between the life of the mother and that of the child, it is up to the individuals concerned to make that decision.

Adoption and Foster Care:

Every effort is made to assist the natural parent(s) to care for their children and to preserve, to the extent possible, the integrity of the family. If custodial care by others is necessary, the best physical, emotional, and spiritual environment is desirable and encouraged.

Advance Directives:

Jehovah's Witnesses carry on their person an Advance Medical Directive/Release that directs no blood transfusions be given under any circumstances, while releasing physicians/hospitals of responsibility for any damages that might be caused by the refusal of blood. When entering the hospital, release forms should be signed that state matters similarly and deal more specifically with the hospital care needed.

Burial of a Fetus:

The decision is a personal one to be made by the couple or the woman involved.

Child Discipline, Neglect, and Abuse:

Child neglect or abuse has no justification. Discipline in the sense of instruction, training, and balanced correction are vital in molding the lives of young children. The Bible speaks approvingly of using the "rod" of parental authority in correction of children, which may include appropriate but moderate physical chastisement at times.—Proverbs 13:24; 29:15, 17.

Circumcision:

Under Christian law, whether one is or is not circumcised has no spiritual value (1 Corinthians 7:19). For an infant, this is a personal matter for the parents to decide.

Decision-making and Treatment Information:

The patient (or parents/guardians of young children) should be fully informed on diagnosis, prognosis, and treatment recommendations so that informed health care decisions can be made. Parents have the natural and legal right to make such decisions for their children. In a rare emergent situation where doctors may feel the need to get a court order to impose medical care which the parents have not consented to (such as administering a blood transfusion), the parents should be informed of such intended action as early as possible, so that they can be represented in court also.

Dietary Laws and Beliefs:

Christians are required to abstain from eating blood and meat of animals from which blood has not properly been drained (Acts 15:28,29). Aside from this Bible injunction, there is no restriction on what is to be eaten.

Dissection and Autopsies:

Unless there is compelling reason, such as when an autopsy is required by a governmental agency, Jehovah's Witnesses generally prefer that the body of a beloved relative not be subjected to a postmortem dissection. The appro-priate relative(s) can decide if a limited autopsy is advisable to determine cause of death, etc.

Handicapping Conditions (Birth Defects):

See comments under "Prolongation of Life and Right to Die."

Immunoglobulins, Vaccines:

The religious understanding of Jehovah's Witnesses does not absolutely prohibit the use of minor blood fractions such as albumin, immune globulins, and hemophiliac preparations. Each Witness must decide individually whether he can accept these. Accepting vaccines from a nonblood source is a medical decision to be made by each one.

"Living Will"/Durable Power of Attorney for Medical Decisions:

Each patient will decide what is appropriate for him/her according to his/her circumstances and the provisions of the law. See "Decision-making and Treatment Information."

Organ Donation and Transplantation:

While the Bible specifically forbids consuming blood, no Biblical command pointedly forbids the taking in of tissue or bone from another human. There-fore, whether to accept an organ transplant is a personal, medical decision. The same would be true of organ donation.

Prolongation of Life and Right to Die:

Life is sacred and the willful taking of life under any health care circumstance would be wrong. For this reason, reasonable and humane effort should be made to sustain and prolong life. However, the Scriptures do not require that extraordinary, complicated, distressing, and costly measures be taken to sustain a person, if such, in the general consensus of the attending physicians, would merely prolong the dying process and/or leave the patient with no quality of life. Any advance directions by the patient that specifically defined what was or was not wanted should be respected.

Religion and Healing Processes (Faith Healing):
Jehovah's Witnesses have faith in God but do not believe in faith healing today. Miraculous healing was God's arrangement for a limited time.

Religious Sacraments, Ordinances, Rituals, and Customs:
Jehovah's Witnesses do not have special rituals that are to be performed for the sick or for those dying. Every reasonable effort should be made to provide medical assistance, comfort, and spiritual care needed by the sick patient.

Use of Alcohol, Narcotics, and Medications:
Moderate use of wine and other alcoholic beverages is not condemned by the Bible, but drunkenness is (1 Timothy 5:23; Deuteronomy 14:26; Ephesians 5:18). Similarly, Bible principles of moderation and respect for one's life and mental faculties would rule out taking drugs for

"highs" and thrills or to produce a form of drunkenness. The taking of mind-altering medication and drugs, including narcotics for severe pain, under the supervision of a physician, would be a matter for personal decision, though one would not want to resort too quickly or without good cause to drugs that were addictive or hallucinatory if other effective methods of treatment were available or if endurance of temporary pain would be the wise and preferable course.

Use of Blood, Blood Products:

Jehovah's Witnesses believe that blood transfusion is forbidden by Biblical passages such as: "Only flesh with its soul—its blood—you must not eat" (Genesis 9:3,4); "[You must] pour its blood out and cover it with dust" (Leviticus 17:13,14); and "Abstain from . . . fornication and from what is strangled and from blood" (Acts 15:19-21) While these verses are not stated in medical terms, Witnesses view them as ruling out transfusion of whole blood, packed red blood cells, white blood cells, plasma, and platelets. However, Witnesses' religious understanding does not absolutely prohibit the use of minor blood fractions, such as albumin, clotting factors, and immune globulins. See "Immunoglobulins, Vaccines."

Refusing blood does not make Jehovah's Witnesses anti-medicine. There are many effective nonblood medical alternatives to homologous blood. For example, nonblood volume expanders are acceptable, and re-infusion of their own blood is permitted by many Witnesses when the blood is not stored and when the equipment is arranged in a circuit that is constantly linked to the patient's circulatory system.

Hospital Protocol for Treating Jehovah's Witnesses

REVIEW nonblood medical alternatives and do not treat the patient with any transfusion, including that of homologous blood.

CONSULT with other doctors at the same facility experienced in nonblood management.

CONTACT the local Hospital Liaison Committee of Jehovah's Witnesses to locate experienced and cooperative doctors at other facilities to consult in alternative care.

TRANSFER the patient, if necessary, to cooperative doctors or facility *before* the patient's condition deteriorates.

IN A RARE SITUATION, if the above steps have been exhausted and governmental intervention is deemed necessary, the patient, the parents, or the guardian should be notified as soon as possible of such intended action.

Reference Materials:

Publications:

Jehovah's Witnesses, *Unitedly Doing God's Will Worldwide*.

Jehovah's Witnesses, *Proclaimers of God's Kingdom*.

Videos:

The Organization Behind the Name.

Purple Triangles (The history of concentration camp suffering during World War II).

A Seventh-Day Adventist View on Death and Dying

Milton L. Perry

Overview of the Seventh-Day Adventists:

Seventh-Day Adventists share many basic beliefs held by most Christians. They accept the authority of the Old and New Testaments. They argue that Christ's death was, "provisionally and potentially for all men," yet efficacious only for those who avail themselves of its benefits. Two other points distinguish the Adventists from other Christians:

1. They observed the seventh day rather than the first day of the week as the Sabbath, and

2. They avoid eating meat and taking narcotics and stimulants, which they consider to be harmful, and they maintain that these are based upon the broad theological consideration that the body is a temple to the holy spirit and should be protected.

William Miller (1782–1849) was one of the founders of the Adventists. While an officer in the

U.S. Army in the War of 1813 Miller had become a skeptic. After a conversion, he began to study the books of Daniel and Revelation and to preach as a Baptist. He was encouraged in his views by a number of clergymen, including Episcopalians and Methodists, and he promptly found himself with many followers.

These were basically an interdenominational movement following the great awakening of the 1840s. Miller, basing his study on the prophetic interpretation of the book of Daniel, said that there was to be an examination of all of the names in the book of life. Only after this would be completed would Christ appear and begin his millennial reign. He held that Christ's advent was, "Personal, visible, audible, bodily, glorious and eminent."

Scenario:

Feeling cold and empty, she sat on the floor facing the wall. The last 48 hours left her in terror and confusion. Her heart cried out for answers: "Why God!? Why would anybody want to kill my children? Why must I lose them to death?"

When Joy and her husband, George, returned home from bingo, they found that their home had become a frantic crime scene. The yard glowed with flashing, red lights emanating from police cars and ambulances. Someone killed their two teenage sons and two young daughters. Like all such crimes, it was senseless and devastating.

In desperation her inner self screamed out to God: "Please, God, hear me! I can't live without my kids. I just can't survive without them. I'm nothing without them." As her thoughts intensified, she ached to know the truth about death, and what happened after death. Were they in heaven? Or someplace else? Would she ever see them again?

The Afterlife and Its Meaning:

As she sat on the floor facing the wall, a peaceful calmness came over her. "You don't have to lose them," a voice seemed to say. "They are in My hands, and I am with you. I will give you My strength. I will help you to be strong enough."

An answer, an assurance, came to her in that soft, quiet voice: "You will be with them again. You have not lost them. You are only separated from them for a little while. It has all been taken care of. The answers you seek, I will show you in My Book. I have written it all down for you."[1]

Next to birth, death is the most common experience of mankind. It is also life's greatest mystery. Answers to that mystery do not come experientially; rather they come by way of philosophies and/or theologies. As Joy Swift came to realize, assurance in the face of death comes not from human reasoning, but from the Word of God. All human wisdom must be subjected to the authority of Scripture. Bible truths are the norm by which all other ideas must be tested. "All scripture

---

[1] Joy Swift, *They're All Dead, Aren't They* (Boise, ID: Pacific Press Publishing Association, 1986), 73–75.

is given by inspiration of God, and is profitable for doctrine."[2]

The doctrine on the state of the dead, and its corollary, the resurrection, as held by Seventh-Day Adventists, is gleaned from the unified teachings of the Old and New Testaments. As succinctly stated in the fundamental beliefs of the church:

> "The wage of sin is death. But God, who alone is immortal, will grant eternal life to His redeemed. Until that day death is an unconscious state for all people. When Christ, who is our life, appears, the resurrected righteous and the living righteous will be glorified and caught up to meet their Lord. The second resurrection, the resurrection of the unrighteous, will take place a thousand years later."[3]

This doctrine is often referred to by polemicists as "soul-sleep." It is based on the inferences of Paul in his discussion of the resurrection. In First Thessalonians he refers to the resurrection of the

---

[2] 2 Timothy 3:16, KJV.

[3] *Seventh-Day Adventist Church Manual* (Silver Spring, MD: General Conference of Seventh-Day Adventists, 1990), 31. This doctrinal statement based on Romans 6:23; 1 Timothy 6:15, 16; Ecclesiastes 9:5, 6; Psalm 146:3, 4; John 11:11–14; Colossians 3:4; 1 Corinthians 15:51–54; 1 Thessalonians 4:13–17; John 5:28, 29; Revelation 20:1–10.

saints who have "fallen asleep";[4] and in First
Corinthians he reminds the church that "we will not
all sleep" clearly a reference to the dead saints who
will be raised at the second coming of Christ.[5] Jesus
more directly referred to death as a sleep just prior
to the resurrections of Lazarus[6] and of the daughter
of Jairus.[7]   As in sleep, death, as attested to in
scripture, is a state of unconsciousness. The dead
know nothing[8]; they praise not God[9]; nor are they
aware of the presence of their loved ones.[10]

In the light of such doctrinal understanding of
scripture, Seventh-Day Adventists reject the idea
that their departed loved ones are in heaven with
God or watching over them as angels.   Such
suggestions bring no comfort to an Adventist at the
time of the death of a loved one. At best such ideas
are accepted with a degree of tolerance.

Wherein, then, does a Seventh-Day Adventist

---

[4] 1 Thessalonians 4:13–15. Three times in this passage Paul
refers to the dead who will be raised in the resurrection as
having "fallen asleep."

[5] 1 Corinthians 15:51. Paul's emphasis here is that the dead do
not receive immortality until the trumpet call of the resurrection
at the second coming of Christ. Once again note that he refers
to death as a sleep.

[6] Matthew 9:24.

[7] John 11:1–15.

[8] Ecclesiastes 9:5–6; Psalm 146:4.

[9] Psalm 115:17; Isaiah 38:18.

[10] Job 14:21; 7:10.

find comfort at the time of death? As the concept of "soul sleep" is presented in the story of the death of Lazarus, so here too one finds Christ's method for comforting the mourning. Jesus directed the attention of a grief-stricken Martha to the hope of the resurrection. He told her, "Your brother will rise again." He then proceeded to identify himself as "the resurrection and the life." Martha's attention was drawn away from the present grief to the future hope of being with her brother once more.[11]

The grieving Thessalonians were approached in a similar way by the apostle Paul. He told them that he did not want them "to be ignorant about those who fall asleep, or to grieve like the rest of men, who have no hope." He pointed their attention away from the present sorrow to the future hope of the second coming of Christ and of the resurrection. He then talked of reuniting with their loved ones: "After that, we who are still alive and are left will be caught up together with them in the clouds to meet the Lord in the air. And so we will be with the Lord forever." The certainty of the second advent of the Lord, the resurrection of the dead, and the reuniting with loved ones are beliefs that Paul presented as comfort, or encouragement, in the face of death.[12]

---

[11] John 11:23–28.

[12] 1 Thessalonians 4:13–18. Paul tells his followers to "comfort" or "encourage" each other with these words. In 1 Corinthians 15:20–23, 51–55, Paul points out that mankind will return to life only at the second coming of Christ, and that it is then that man receives an imperishable body and immortality.

To Seventh-day Adventists who believe in the imminent second advent of the Lord and Savior, Jesus Christ, death can be seen as a transitory absence from their loved ones. Here is where comfort can be found.

It is often expressed among Christians that death came because God needed "the loved ones" to be with Him in heaven. Adventists find it hard to understand how anyone can find comfort in such an idea. Instead of being words of comfort, the concept presents a selfish God who took away a son or a daughter, a wife or a husband, at His whim and depriving one of their presence. In this, God is viewed as the author of death and making it his ordained means of transition from being human to becoming spirit; and that death may come in any one of a multitude of tragic ways. Is God the author of death and suffering? Such a view is foreign to scripture.

Scripture gives us a picture of God as the creator of life—one who loves His creatures and desires their greatest good. He created man in His own image and assured man of eternal life within a harmonious relationship with Himself. It was a breaking off from that harmonious relationship that brought sin and death upon all mankind.[13] Into God's perfect creation came the alien experiences of sin and death, for "the wage of sin is death." Even the final destruction of the wicked is seen as God's

---

[13] Genesis 1:27; 2:16–17; 3:1–19; Romans 5:12.

"strange work . . . his alien task."[14] Yet God's great desire for humanity is the gift of immortality. Eternal life is an unmerited gift that He will give to all who will be willing to receive it within a renewed harmonious relationship.[15] Seventh-Day Adventists see death and tragedy not as God's ordained will, rather as that of an enemy.

The Meaning and Value of Illness and Suffering:

Death does not always strike suddenly. The tragedy may well be in the long, lingering anticipation of the surety of death. In such terminal situations, Seventh-Day Adventists take great comfort in the Biblical promises of strength[16] and the future home of the saints.[17] As the life forces ebb away, and the frustration of increasing weakness takes its hold, one must be reminded that in weakness God gives strength. Paul came to this realization when the Lord pointed out to him in his weakness that, "My grace is sufficient for you, for my power is made perfect in weakness." While God may not see it in the best interest to heal a terminally ill person, He never fails to provide His strength and comfort to that person when asked according to His promises. Ellen G. White, a revered pioneer leader

---

[14] Isaiah 28:21.

[15] Romans 6:23.

[16] Romans 8:35–39; Psalm 23; Matthew 11:28–30; Isaiah 40:28–31; Psalm 46:1–7.

[17] John 14:1–3; Revelation 21:1–5.

of the Seventh-Day Adventist Church, wrote concerning the spiritual struggle of the dying: "Often your mind may be clouded because of pain. Then do not try to think. You know that Jesus loves you. He understands your weakness. You may do His will by simply resting in His arms."[18]

Rituals Around Death:

The health professional and other caregivers of a terminally ill Seventh-Day Adventist should be aware that Adventists believe in anointing the sick. Anointing should not be seen as a demand that God heal the person; rather, it places the individual within the will of God, advances the harmonious relationship with God, and promotes spiritual and mental health. The Epistle of James directs: "Is any one of you sick? He should call the elders of the church to pray over him and anoint him with oil in the name of the Lord."[19] Caregivers would do well to encourage the terminally ill, or their family, to request anointing.

To Call for Assistance When Patients are Acutely Ill or Dying:

Like other Christians, most Seventh-Day Adventists like to have their pastor notified when facing death. It may not always be possible for the

---

[18] Ellen G. White, *The Ministry of Healing* (Mountain View, CA: Pacific Press Publishing Association, 1905), 251.

[19] James 5:14, NIV.

Adventist patient to call his own pastor, and family members may not be church members. In such cases, the caregiver may bear the responsibility of contacting the local church and pastor. In denominationally administered hospitals, that may be as simple as calling the hospital chaplain's office. In other cases, the caregiver should check in the yellow pages of the phone directory under the heading of "Churches" and the subheading "Seventh-Day Adventist."

Death is always hard to understand, and dealing with it is difficult. Yet as caregivers take the time to understand the viewpoint from which their Seventh-Day Adventist patients approach death, greater comfort and encouragement can be given that may make a difference to the dying and their family.

The Perspective of Hinduism

Debasis Bagchi

An Overview of Hinduism:

H induism is the oldest religion in the world and is the faith of over four-fifths of the diverse peoples of the vast subcontinent of India, of the people of Nepal and Bali (Indonesia), and of millions of Indians who have migrated overseas. Many ancient cultures and religions in Southeast Asia have been greatly influenced by the Hindu cultural ethos.

Hinduism totally permeates the life of every Hindu from the moment of his birth, be he or she a scholar or an illiterate. It is for this reason that it is often said that Hinduism is not just a religion but a way of life.

The word *Hindu* is of geographic origin and was derived from the name originally given to the people settled on the river *Sindhu*. Scholars call this the Brahmanical faith, for to attain the Brahman or the Universal Soul is the aim of all Hindu thought.

The history of the Hindus, as we know it today, goes back more than 5,000 years. Hindus believe that their religion is without beginning or end and is a continuous process. Science today accepts that there may be other worlds in the Universe, each with its own laws. Hindus have always held this view.

The Goals of Life in Hinduism:

Hindu scriptures describe four principal goals of Hindu life. According to the Hindu religious teachings, the highest goal of human life is to attain *Moksha* or Absolution, i.e., freedom from transmigration of the soul. The mere existence of an individual in this world is simply a means for attaining this goal *Moksha*. However, one cannot attain Moksha without fulfilling other personal and social obligations. *Moksha*, the last and supreme goal, could only be attained upon fulfilling three other goals.

1. *DHARMA*—Righteousness
2. *ARTHA*—Wealth
3. *KAMA*—Pleasures
4. *MOKSHA*—Spiritual Perfection

Hindu scriptures declare that an individual is made of four parts: *Shrine*—Physical Body, *Manas*—Mind, *Bhudhi*—Intellect, and the *Atman*—Self or Soul. To maintain the physical body and to satisfy the needs of the family and dependents, an individual needs worldly properties—*Artha*, i.e., money; to satisfy the mind, intellect and desires—*Kama*, i.e., pleasures or lust; however, to satisfy material needs and natural desires, one must still adhere to the most important and the first goal—Dharma, the righteous living. When these goals end, aims are well practiced and attained, then comes the supreme and ultimate goal of *Moksha*.

The Scriptures of the Hindus:

Hinduism is not based on any single book or on the words of any single teacher or prophet. The following are the most referred Hindu Scriptures:

1. *THE SHRUTIS/VEDAS:* The first set of books, which are the primary authority or the very soul of Hinduism, are known as *Shruti*, meaning that which has been heard or revealed.

2. *THE SMRITIS:* The second set are the *Smritis*, meaning that which is remembered. Unlike the *Shrutis,* which are of Divine origin, the *Smritis* are human compositions which regulate and guide individuals in their daily conduct, and a list of codes and rules governing the actions of the individual, the community, society, and the nation.

3. *THE EPICS:* The great *Epics* of Hinduism are the *Ramayana*, the *Mahabharata*, the *Yogavasistha*, and the *Harivamsa*. These *Epics* are also called *Suhrit Samhitas* or friendly compositions, as they teach the greatest of truths in an easy and friendly way without taxing the mind, as the language is simple and the contents easily understood.

4. *THE PURANAS:* There are 18 *Puranas* of which the *Bhagvata*, *Vishnu*, and *Markendaya Puranas* are most popular, and 18 subsidiary or *Upa Puranas*. The *Puranas* are not meant for the scholar, the intellectual, or the spiritually

evolved, but consist of tales which convey the truths of the *Vedas* and *Dharma Shastras* in the form of short stories. Told to children, to the simple villager and illiterate peasant, these imaginative stories have formed the very basis of the religious education of the ordinary people and help to teach them simple but fundamental truths of religion and morality, of what is right and wrong in behavior.

5. *THE AGAMAS*: *Agamas* lay down the separate theological disciplines and doctrines for the worship of particular deities.

6. *THE DARSHANAS:* These scriptures highlight the six *Darshanas* (meaning visions) which are schools of philosophy. These are for the intellectuals and the scholars who have six main schools of philosophic thought to guide them.

The Three Paths to Reach the Brahman or the Absolute:

To achieve this spiritual union with the Supreme Soul (Brahman), there are believed to be three main paths: Bhakti Yoga (through Bhakti or devotion), Karma Yoga (by Karma or action), and Jnana Yoga (the path of wisdom or spiritual enlightenment).

The Perspective of Hinduism on the Meaning of Illness and Suffering:

One of the basic beliefs of Hinduism is the law of Karma or Action, the law of cause and effect. It is explained by the saying, "As we sow, so shall we reap." A farmer cannot leave his fields fallow and expect a crop of wheat. Nor can he sow tomatoes and expect a crop of mangoes. Similarly every good thought, word, or deed begets a similar reaction which affects our next lives, and every unkind thought, harsh word, and evil deed comes back to harm us in this life or the next. Hindus believe that *Unfair Karma* is one of the main bases of illness or suffering. However, *Ayurveda* has repeatedly indicated that irregular lifestyle, uncontrolled food habits, and overstress can lead to various diseases, distress, and disorders in humans. Several therapies including surgery have been suggested to heal various diseased conditions in *Ayurveda*.

The View of the Value of Suffering:

Hindus believe in the cycle of birth, death, and rebirth, known as Samsara, and every soul must go through this cycle of births and deaths before the soul attains *Moksha* or Absolution. Only the soul which reaches True Perfection in this life becomes one with the Brahman and is not born again. We do not accept that the Great God would be cruel enough to create the great inequalities that exist in the world. He would not create one child beloved of happy parents, another who is handicapped or blind or suffering from a permanent disorder, and a third who is unwanted, born to impoverished parents and left hungry. The inequalities of life are understandable only when we realize that they are of man's own *Karma* or Actions and not of God's creation. Each one of us at birth is the result of our past life. Our birth in this life is determined by the good and bad thoughts, words, and deeds of a previous birth. Thus *Unfair Karma* will lead to illness and suffering in the same or next life.

The View of Hinduism on Afterlife and Its Meaning:

According to Hinduism, the ultimate goal is for the individual soul in each one of us, known as the *Atma*, to attain the *Brahman* or the Universal Holy Soul. All souls are not able to achieve this happy state even after death. On the other hand, most of us die only to be born again and again. This cycle of birth, death, and rebirth is called *Samsara*, and every soul must go through this cycle of births and deaths before it attains *Moksha* or Absolution or Liberation. Based on a True *Karma* or Action, only the soul which attains perfection in this life becomes one with the Brahman and is not born again. This doctrine of *Samsara* or rebirth is also called the *theory of reincarnation* or the *transmigration of the soul* and is a basic tenet of Hinduism. The *Great Hindu Upanishads* compare the passage of the soul to a caterpillar which climbs a blade of grass, leaves it, and jumps onto a new one. Just as a man changes worn-out garments and wears new ones, so does the soul cast away one body and take on another.

However, according to Hinduism, we do not carry the burden of our previous lives in our consciousness, though we do in our subconscious minds. The birth of a musical genius in an unmusical family, or of great scholars and artists whose education and environment do not explain their achievements, are a few evidences of the spill-over from previous births.

The Key Terms and Vocabulary That Nurses, Physicians, and Clergy Might Use in Dealing with a Patient and His Family at Times of Acute Illness and Death:

Most individuals will wish to perform a single or a set of prayers. Since very few health care providers may be able to go through all the prayers, some may be willing to chant "OM" (Om. Peace. Peace. Peace).

The View of the Hindu Religion on Visiting the Sick:

The visitors, including relatives and friends, pray to God before and after visiting a sick person. Hindu visitors also extend their wholehearted support to the patient and his or her family. Most of the time the Hindu visitors, friends, and relatives perform a joint prayer to The God along with the patient. Sometimes the visitors read chapters from the Holy Book of Bhagavad Gita. The main purpose of this visit is to extend moral, economic, and spiritual support to the patient.

The Hindu Practice Regarding the Postmortem Preparation of the Body If Death Occurs:

Nowadays an autopsy is to some extent accepted by the Hindus, although it is still not very well accepted in villages in India. Cremation is the ultimate ritual of the body after death occurs.

Assistance When Physicians, Nurses, Social Workers, or Hospital Clergy Need Information about Dealing with Patients of the Hindu Religion, Particularly If They are Acutely Ill or Dying:

If a patient wants to see a Hindu priest, please contact the local Hindu Temple. Most large cities have a Temple, listed in the telephone book Yellow Pages under "Churches," or "Religious Organizations."

In Omaha or rural Nebraska or surrounding states, contact the Hindu Temple, 13010 Arbor Street, Omaha, NE 68144. Phone: (402) 697-8546.

The Hindu Temple is open on Saturdays and Sundays from 10:30 AM to 1:00 PM. Please feel free to contact Dr. D. Bagchi (402) 496-0410; Dr. S. Joshi (402) 330-1935; Dr. A. V. Subbaratnam (402) 330-7184; or Mrs. Ambika Nair (402) 330-2398 for all other days and times.

The Plains Indians' Perspective on Acute Illness and Death

Marlene EchoHawk

Overview:

There are over 500 federally recognized tribes in the United States. With the vast number of tribes there is also a diversity of culture and traditions associated with each tribe. Some tribes are similar in tradition and belief systems. One of the tribal groupings that is similar has been called the Plains Indians or those tribes that lived and hunted in the area designated as the Great Plains.

The Great Plains is generally considered to be in the central part of the United States. Beginning with North Dakota, extending south as far as Texas, the area west of the Mississippi River extending further west to the Rocky Mountains.

The Plains Indian tribes, to name a few, are Cheyenne, Comanche, Arapaho, Kiowa, Crow, Omaha, Ote-Missouria, Osage, Quapaw, Ponca, Kaw, Iowa, Pawnee, Arikara, Mandan, Hidatsa, Sioux, Shoshone, and others.

While the various Plains tribes spoke different dialects, they learned to communicate by sign language and some also became fluent in the various dialects. Some of the dialects were similar enough that tribes could communicate verbally. This holds true even up to the present time. Some tribes are still able to communicate through the similarity of their dialects.

The last of the "Indian Wars" was fought in the Northern Plains. History informs us of the massacre of defenseless Native Americans carried out at Wounded Knee, the Battle of The Little Big Horn and the defeat of General Custer by the Plains Indians. There is no need to recite what most of us have learned either through our history books, or in the case of Native Americans, through the recitation of our oral history.

Unfortunately, as in all wars, the emotional scars and psychological trauma endured by all those involved take many years to heal. Throughout the Great Plains and, possibly throughout the country, there is a need to recognize and understand the process of healing "old wounds" as it relates to Plains Indian tribes.

The author hopes to convey useful information regarding how the Plains Indians cope with acute illness and death.

Background:

There is the belief among Plains Indians, as with most Native American tribes, that there is a close relationship between the physical side of one's existence and the nonphysical side of a person's existence. There must be a balance between the physical and social with the mental and spiritual in order for a person to function at greatest potential, or to remain whole.

There is a recognition of the finite existence of man's physical being. The extent to which an individual respects the wholeness of life will be reflected in the individual's physical nature.

When a person is faced with a serious illness and must endure great physical suffering there is the belief that the individual is out of harmony with his or her whole state of being. Therefore, the focus of healing, or help, will come by giving attention to the physical, but utilizing the other components of his or her total existence: physical, social, mental, and spiritual.

Plains' Indians View on the Value of Suffering:

The main value of suffering, if it can be called a value, is to alert the individual that some part, or parts, of their existence is out of balance. This refers to what was mentioned above: the physical, social, mental, or spiritual.

In the physical realm there can be many causes, as health care providers and traditional healers are aware. To use some examples, it may relate to poor nutritional practices, not getting enough rest or enough exercise, etc. In the social area it may relate to poor relationships with friends and/or relatives, or community members, or, vice versa, overextending one's self in relationships and "partying" too much and too often, or a death of a close friend or relative. In the mental area there could be depression related to some loss through death, or job loss, moving to a new location and a loss of contact with friends and relatives. In the spiritual area there may be little attention given to the spiritual side of one's existence: neglecting prayers and meditation or lack of having been taught by parents or elders regarding one's spirituality.

The components of what is believed to make up the whole person are, at any given movement, in dynamic interaction. A single component does not operate separately.

Plains Indians' Views on Visiting the Sick:

The main purpose in visiting the sick is to give support to the person who is ill. The support will be given through the physical and social presence of visiting. Also, through encouraging the patient to have a positive mental attitude to regaining health and, very importantly, to either offer a prayer for and with the patient, or to assure the patient that prayers are being said on the patient's behalf.

Even though the patient is being hospitalized due to a physical problem, the visitors will recognize the need to encourage the patient psychologically. The psychological intervention will give attention to the wholeness of the patient and remind the patient of what that means.

The meaning of physical wholeness means that we are able to use all of our senses that we have been endowed with. Therefore, the patient will be reminded through the sense of sight—the physical presence of the visitors, the sense of hearing—talking and maybe singing of prayers for the patient, the sense of taste—bringing specific food or healing herbal medicine to the patient—the sense of smell—burning cedar or sweetgrass for the patient to remind him or her of his or her spiritual nature utilizing the sense of smell—and the sense of touch—this is awakened through a gentle handshake or hug, when appropriate, for the patient.

Many times health care providers are not sensitive to the restorative powers of social interaction, however limited that may be in a hospital setting. Plains Indians believe that even patients who are comatose are mentally and spiritually cognizant, and will talk and pray for them even if the patient is unable to physically respond. Plains Indians, perhaps as most Native Americans, do not always feel welcome in a hospital setting. Sometimes it is as if health care providers want to intrude on visitors' time, limit the visit, or control how the visit is carried out. Of course, visitors must be made aware of hospital rules and policies, but other than that, if visitors are made to feel welcome and allowed some private time with the patient, a good supportive network could evolve.

In general, people visiting patients in the hospital setting feel uneasy. It would be nice if someone from the hospital staff could, at some point, give welcome assurance to visitors that their visit is appreciated. Hospital staff are so vital and their workload is heavy; maybe a nicely worded brochure would suffice.

Plains Indians View of Afterlife:
As mentioned, Plains Indians recognize the

physical as well as the nonphysical realm of man's existence. There is understanding and acceptance of the finiteness of one's physical existence. However, there is also the belief that the spiritual nature of a person is infinite.

Plains Indians view the time spent in the physical state as a "preparation" for the spiritual world from which all life originated and will return. This is what the teaching of Plains Indians regarding "respect for life" is all about. Respect for life in all its forms, plants, animals, and all of creation is how Plains Indians are to conduct themselves throughout their physical lifetimes.

Also, as mentioned earlier, when an individual is out of balance in his or her life, then the imbalance will be manifested in a physical manner which is intertwined to the wholeness of an individual.

Each person has the responsibility to value the gift of life, but also has the freedom to decide when to leave the physical state and return to the spiritual world. If family and friends understand that the patient has made the decision to "give up on this physical life" and to spiritually "go on" they can be supportive of the patient's decision. Generally, this might happen if the person is old and may have spoken of himself as a "burden" or not physically able to enjoy the quality of life that he or she once enjoyed.

If the person is young and speaks of death or wanting to die then family and friends consider that to be extremely critical because the person has not given life a chance. Family and friends will try to influence the person to participate in life and to not choose death. There may be a traditional ceremony held for the person or suggestions offered for the person to obtain help through a western mental health program or both types of help may be provided.

In any event there will generally be a great deal of emotion displayed by family and friends. Family members will want to stay close to the sick relative even if they are resigned to the knowledge that the patient is too ill to physically survive. Family members may rely heavily on a spiritual leader to give emotional support to the whole family.

Suggestions for Health Care Providers:

It cannot be emphasized too strongly that being honest and forthright in letting family know the status of their loved one who is acutely ill or near death is all important. The family will already have some intuitive knowledge of the status and will, most likely, appreciate the honesty of the health care provider.

Health care providers' knowledge that there may be specific rituals or traditions that the family would like to carry out and the acknowledgment of the family's wishes is greatly appreciated. Privacy is also appreciated, along with the information that if there is anything the staff can help with, the family is free to call for that help.

The above are just common sense suggestions, but Native Americans have been seriously neglected when it comes to spiritual or religious practices in the hospital setting.

In the first place, Plains Indians are most at home with their spiritual practices within their own community environment and will not want to engage in rituals in a hospital setting. However, just to know that their traditions will be respected and honored can be of great comfort to the family.

A very common practice among Plains Indian families facing a relative's acutely ill situation is to burn sweetgrass or cedar. If this presents any kind of safety hazard then this can be explained to the family. Flames close to an oxygen tank or something of that nature that has validity will be acceptable. Prohibiting the practice without giving an explanation is considered to be insensitive.

Hospital staff's sensitivity to the Plains Indians traditions is all that will be necessary. If death is imminent, the family will want to maintain an around-the-clock vigil. They will want to know if they are welcome. Have a hospital staff person let the family know the situation. If, for some valid reason, the family cannot be allowed in the very room with the patient, then let the family know where they are welcome to wait. Or, if it is wise to set a limit of only one family member allowed in the patient's room, then explain the rationale to the family. All this takes valuable time, but gives the family support and will gain their respect. If the actual provider is unable to give this kind of support, the family will understand. The support can come from the hospital clergy or other hospital staff person.

Urban Indian Centers in metropolitan areas can be a source of information on how to locate other Plains' Indians.

Plains Indians' Postmortem Preparation of the Body:

Once a family member or friend has died then it is essential that someone remain with the deceased at all times for a period of four days. The belief is that the spirit of the deceased is still around and will visit all the places that were visited during the physical existence. This is a very sacred time and Plains Indians who still practice their traditions will remain close by. Care must be taken by hospital staff to not interpret this behavior as a pathological reluctance to leave the deceased.

Tradition requires that the body be prepared in a certain way which can only be carried out by those who have the authority to utilize the ritual. There is current knowledge of the preparation of bodies in the Western fashion. There is generally no problem with this. Sacred rituals will generally be carried out after the hospital has released the body of the deceased, and again family members or friends will want to remain close by.

In this current period when Plains Indians have other religious beliefs besides the traditional belief system, an autopsy may be allowed. The request can be made of the family and permission may be granted. However, those adhering to traditional custom will not permit an autopsy to be carried out on the body. An autopsy is considered to be a form of desecration of the body.

At the time of death it is appropriate to express grief through crying. Plains Indians are not reluctant to express their grief through shedding of tears and it is actually expected. This may be too much for non-Indians to witness and they will make attempts to inhibit the legitimate expression of feelings. Hospital staff need only ask themselves if it is their own discomfort or is the grief truly upsetting other patients? Most hospitals have a family room for the grief-stricken to remain until they are composed enough to leave on their own.

Conclusion:

As we live in closer and closer proximity to those of other cultures, it is important to become sensitive to the belief system of other cultures. Plains Indians have been suppressed in the expression of their traditional belief system. This is true for other Native Americans as well.

This author appreciates the opportunity to provide information inasmuch as the information relates to Plains Indians.

Hopefully, the sensitivity of health care providers will be enhanced to some degree by this information.

The Diné Perspective: To Walk in Beauty

Charlene Avery

Overview:

To walk in a constant state of beauty is the Diné (Navajo) person's highest aspiration. This achievement marks one's adherence to Navajo "religious" principles and denotes a healthy, balanced state of mind, body, spirit, and universe. Such is the worldview of the Diné, meaning "The People" in the language otherwise known as Navajo.

The Diné originated in the north according to the story of Creation. At the time of Diné Creation, a proscribed life way or religion was taught to The People on how to maintain order and harmony within the universe. This life way is the basis for Navajo wellness. To maintain excellent health, one must live in accordance with the life ways which suggest how The People can maintain mental, physical, and spiritual well-being.

Anthropologically the Diné are classified as an Athabascan group with origins also from the north. Current reservation boundaries extend from northeastern Arizona to northwestern New Mexico and into southeastern Utah. The tribal population consists of more than 200,000 people, of which approximately half reside on the Navajo Reservation. The other half of the population resides in reservation border towns and throughout the United States. There are hundreds and thousands of Navajos located in the major cities of the U.S. Some of the largest off-reservation groups of Navajos are in Los Angeles, Phoenix, Albuquerque, Denver, Chicago, Washington, D.C., and New York City.

Cultural practices remain rich and are evident throughout Navajo land and wherever Navajo people are located. Clan and kinship ties determine various aspects of Diné social organization as does the matriarchal structure of Navajo life. Cultural expression occurs in many forms both traditional and contemporary. Governmental structure parallels that of the U.S. government and Navajo law exists as the Tribal Code. Economic development focuses on utilization of natural resources.

Through intermarriage and the prevalence of Christianity, some Navajos have adopted Christianity and other religions. Some Navajos have adopted non-Navajo religions exclusively, some have added other belief systems to their own which they are comfortable merging, some practice Christianity on Sundays and otherwise follow Navajo beliefs, and some freely attend Navajo ceremonials and otherwise follow Christian beliefs. The practice of sending Native American children to distant mission schools of various faiths included

Navajo children. This experience has had different effects on The People—some converted to the new lifestyle and others reject non-Navajo ways. Frequently the Diné will make clear their preferences.

Diné history in relation to native-white relations is tragic as it is for every other tribal group in America. Yet the Diné have survived like no other—with culture virtually intact and the means to excel. Being Diné means being adaptable. Contemporary Diné life is equally complex and variable as traditional life. Contemporary Diné are educated, practicing in fields including medicine, law, engineering, sociology, education, and many others. Nonetheless, many educated tribal members continue to hold closely to traditional beliefs and language usage. Indeed, leadership positions often require command of Diné bizaad, The People's language.

Diné history in relation to the western model of health care is tragic as well. Tuberculosis, influenza, dysentery, and the lack of access to health care to deal with illnesses foreign to the Diné resulted in the deaths of thousands of people. Many Navajos have indeed died at area hospitals in the not-so-distant past. Sometimes death occurred because treatment had not been sought earlier, which in itself was due to the great distances one had to travel; in addition, modern health care resources were very limited in those older days. For these reasons, it is important to allay Diné fears that the hospital is merely "a place to die."

Despite progress within Navajo land, there remain vastly isolated communities where schools are few and where exposure to the outside world is limited. Many of these areas are so remote that employment is severely limited. In these remote areas Navajo is the first and primary language and the practice of traditional ways is especially strong.

Many believe the decreased attention to traditional ways and the trend toward a more modern existence accounts for the changes in the health status of the Navajo. There is increasing obesity, diabetes, cancer, coronary disease, sedentary lifestyles, and even cigarette smoking, which is considered revolting by most Navajos.

Access to modern health care is still difficult and is dominated by the Indian Health Service, a governmental entity similar to the Veterans Administration Hospital system. In more recent health care history, newer hospitals have brought physicians in service for loan payback, culture-curious student and resident physicians, locum tenens physicians to reduce staff shortages, and a general lack of understanding and sensitivity on the part of health care providers to the needs of traditional Diné. Remote hospitals continue with high staff turnover rates and it is well known and expected that one will not have any continuity of care at the reservation hospitals.

Even more frightening is the presence of *Hantavirus* and its rapid death course. The outbreak of this illness underscored in the minds of Diné that the modern world of medicine has little to offer.

The fact that one can appear to have a benign illness yet rapidly become deathly ill places the Navajo person in a dilemma of mistrust of the health care system versus the hope that perhaps modern medicine can save a life in this highly fatal condition.

Fortunately the Navajo traditional medical system continues to exist. Navajo people continue to use medicine men and medicine women for their healing. The traditional medicine approach is used as first-line treatment, as an adjunct to modern care, as an alternative method if no relief is obtained through other means, or not at all. The approach taken depends on the individual and the nature of their illness.

To understand Diné medicine, one must understand that medicine and religion are virtually identical. The central theme is that everything in the universe has life; all things breathe and live and have a spirit and power. Further, all of these beings are interrelated and influence the workings of the universe; each has a role and responsibility for maintaining order within the universe. When disruptions or imbalances occur—whether from unhealthy interactions among the beings, or from negative mental, physical, or spiritual activity—illness results. The disharmony or illness may manifest itself in mental, physical, or spiritual realms as well as within the universe itself.

The restoration of a healthy state is achieved through correction of imbalances. Corrective measures usually involve a ceremony of some type—a simple prayer, use of a medicinal substance, rituals of varying length and intricacy, or other activities such as dances, chants, physical manipulations, sand paintings, and other ceremonial observances.

One finds in traditional Diné medicine many parallels to modern medicine—with specialists, multiple diagnostic modalities, physical treatments, medicines, and referrals. Prevention is key and a heavy emphasis is placed on always thinking good, healthy, beautiful thoughts in order to prevent illness and keep oneself strong.

Visiting the Sick:

Unlike modern medicine, the role of family and community plays a major part in traditional Navajo medicine and is deemed essential to the healing process. The patient and participants/observers become involved in the focusing of positive thoughts and positive prayers on the ailing person; these participants become of one mind in beauty and health. These positive thoughts and prayers become a healing energy force for the Diné patient. Therefore, visitation of sick individuals is not considered harmful in the way that harboring an ill person might be in Diné culture. Clearly, association with negativity has implications for one's health just as focus on positivity has health promotion effects.

Terminal Illness:

Another role for traditional medicine which differs from the modern system is its use to achieve a healthy state of mind and not necessarily a physical cure. Such achievement allows one to be at peace and feel well despite whatever future course one's illness may take. This function is essential for those confronting a terminal illness.

Incorporating Traditional Healing:

Encouraging and accommodating traditional healing methods will go far in improving your treatment of the Navajo patient; compliance, trust, and respect for your methods will heighten. Realize that a patient may delay their surgery or chemo-therapy or other treatment until they have had a traditional blessing to assure their safety through the treatment process. This precaution is a major factor in a patient's follow-up course and should be regarded as an intelligent choice rather than a foolish and inconvenient delay. Proper space and time can usually be readily arranged for the traditional healer who wishes to treat within the hospital: this is not uncommon in many South-western hospitals.

Death:

Understand there may be patient fears of being experimented upon or memory of relatives who died within the modern medical system. Anything that has been touched by death is considered tainted; the patient may then be reluctant or unwilling to have treatment administered at the local hospital. Acknowledge these fears and reassure the patient that medical care has progressed, that student doctors are supervised, that a medicine man performed a cleansing and blessing of the facility recently, etc. Allowing family to accompany the patient may also help.

Decision Making:

The role of females in Navajo society cannot be overemphasized. Because Navajo society is matriarchal, everything in Diné life is centered around the older, dominant female. Property, children, clan relationships, and one's residence are all determined through the female line. In any serious situation confronting a Navajo family, there will be one or more females coming forward to make decisions about their family's well-being. Although the females will in turn consult with other family members including the men, decisions rely most heavily upon the input of the dominant female. In many cases the dominant female is the grandmother or eldest female in an extended family unit.

Ascertain who key decision makers are, as they may not be the patient; reassure and educate the decision maker so they may effectively assist the patient in embarking on a course of treatment. Follow-up care instructions should also be relayed to this person so that compliance can be assured. Although the decision maker is usually the primary caretaker of a seriously ill individual, at times these responsibilities are delegated to another family member. Communicating the patient's needs to the decision maker will usually assure that proper arrangements for care are made.

Suffering:

Suffering, the culmination of unpleasant experiences, is given to the Diné in order to refine problem-solving abilities. Suffering can be considered a manifestation of illness or imbalance with the same potential for complications, if not addressed. Suffering may be caused by external forces such as one person wishing harm upon another. Regardless of its source, like illness and death, suffering is a concept not to be dwelled upon. Rather, suffering should be avoided altogether or relieved as soon as possible.

No particular value is attached to suffering. However, there may be value in the higher reason for the suffering such as overcoming the imbalance, achieving the goal, becoming pain-free, or improving one's health. Like death, hunger, and poverty, suffering is understood as somewhat inevitable and sufferers are sympathized and supported through their healing process.

Affecting Predestination:

Navajos believe one's length of life is predetermined. However, because the universe consists of matter and beings capable of exerting both positive and negative forces on one another, a person's life can be influenced to continue living or to not continue living through these external forces. Such interaction can be as simple as one form or being exerting its thoughts negatively upon another. Conversely, a ceremony can be used to influence the living state more positively.

Serious Prognosis:

Thus, in discussing poor prognostic states with a Navajo person, one would best be advised to discuss a poor prognosis in the third person. In other words, "if someone had this condition . . . " and not "you have this condition." In the former approach, one can then ask the patient what they think of *this* scenario and not what they think of *their* scenario. The patient is then much freer to postulate and give general opinions of what they might advise for such an individual. One's preferences for care can then be clearly deduced from this theoretical discussion and cross checked if necessary.

View of Afterlife:

Among the Diné, there is no afterlife and discussion of death and any such possibilities is frowned upon. The dead state and what becomes of the body and spirit are dark, unknown, and highly undesirable states. Discussion of these states is believed to hasten one's demise. Thinking illness-related thoughts likewise can be sufficient to bring illness upon oneself. A third-person discussion is strongly advised when addressing terminal illness or requesting advance directives to avoid giving the impression that you are "wishing for" or have "assigned" death to the patient.

Postmortem:

Death is, however, acknowledged as inevitable and necessary in the natural law of the Diné. Once death occurs, contact with the deceased is limited to the minimum amount of contact for appropriate and respectful handling of the body. Any contact with the dead person is believed to convey a risk of death to the person handling the deceased. Therefore, ritual cleansing takes place following such contact. In fact, some funeral goers without direct contact will also cleanse ritually afterward. The advent of funeral homes has lessened some of the death anxiety encountered during such times by relieving family members of the burden of direct contact with the dead. Excessive exposure to the deceased's belongings or dwelling is also discouraged. In older times, a dead person's home and belongings were destroyed.

Autopsy:

Autopsies, in general, are not options. Even when faced with a mysterious death families are not likely to consent to an autopsy because death is understood as part of the natural law and autopsy will not reverse this natural order. Autopsies are considered acts of desecration; they also imply a "revisitation," examination, questioning, and overall excessive concentration on the deceased—which are not desirable activities.

Similarly, organ donation is the very rare exception and for an additional reason—Navajo people believe that objects of one's person may be used negatively by others to induce a state of illness or endangerment for the owner. Giving one's organs is a potentially harmful act if one does not know what will be done with the organs in the future, i.e., whether the recipient will live in a good way with those organs or through bad behavior or bad thoughts bring mishap to the donor. Receiving organs may be similarly harmful, for one may receive an item with death directly attached, or from a person who did not live in a balanced state—the organs may then exert damaging effects on the recipient.

Ritualization:

There are other methods to help the Diné patient. If possible, ritualize the prescribed treatment or place it in a cultural context: "take medication before and after tending the sheep"; "pray that the medicine will help you just as if it were a plant medicine." Seek understanding of the plant medicines being used so that adjustments in care may be made; if emetics are being used, adjust medication timing so that medication is retained long enough for absorption; adjust diuretic therapy if a sweat lodge is being planned. Building trust and learning respectfully are necessary if this information is to be shared with you.

Translation:

Use interpreters and discuss openly with them their degree of accuracy in interpreting medical information. Interpreting in Navajo can be a difficult and frustrating procedure due to the descriptiveness and complexity of the Navajo language. Investigate other barriers to care such as limited water supply, no phone access, absent in-home helpers, lack of transportation, etc. On the Navajo Reservation only 15% of homes have telephones.

Clearly, Diné life ranges from traditional to modern and blends of both. For this reason it is important not to make assumptions about the Diné individual or family or group. Some families will be more at ease discussing death issues. Being sincere in your learning efforts about Navajo culture will allow your patient to make the nuances more clear to you. With its many contrasts and juxtapositions within modern society, one can truly describe Diné life as a mosaic. For the Diné, maintaining balance within this mosaic is a lifelong healing journey.

Assistance:

For assistance in addressing the care needs of Navajo patients, the patient and family are the best immediate sources of culture-based information. Otherwise, if on or near the Navajo Reservation, contact a local social services office or Indian Health Service facility. Elsewhere in major cities, the local urban Indian Center will be likely to yield a Diné contact person. The Association of American Indian Physicians can give guidance Monday through Friday at (405) 946-7072.

REFERENCES

Avery, Charlene. "Native American Medicine: Traditional Healing." *Journal of the American Medical Association*, vol. 265, no. 17. May 1, 1991. pp. 2271–2273.

Begay, M.D., Ray & Natonabah, Andy. "1996 Association of American Indian Physicians Cross

Cultural Medicine Workshop," Santa Fe, New Mexico.

Jackson, Dean C. "Comparative Philosophy" Navajo Community College, Tsaile, Arizona (Undated).

Lauber, M.D., Caleb. Navajo family physician. Personal communication. June 18, 1996.

Natonabah, Andy. "Navajo Theories of Illness and Healing." Navajo Community College, Tsaile, Arizona (Undated).

Hispanics in the Southwest U.S.

Delfi Mondragón

Center for Health Policy and Ethics, Creighton University

Overview:

When dealing with Hispanics in the United States, it is important to remember that there is a tremendous variation in this group. It is impossible to categorize cultural responses to illness and death, because Hispanics in the U.S. come from about 63 different countries. It is possible, however, to generalize somewhat about Hispanic groups in various geographic locations. Such groups would be, for example, Mexican Americans in the Southwest, Cuban Americans in Miami, Puerto Ricans in New York City, or various South and Central Americans in large U.S. cities.

It is helpful to know the history of Hispanic Americans, if one wants to understand these patients better: Spain in the 14th century was the most powerful nation in the world, with large and powerful naval forces. They set out to the new world, conquering and occupying indigent peoples' territory from the Canary Islands in the North

131

Atlantic Ocean, most of the Caribbean Islands, most of Central and South America, and in North America—all of Mexico and the territory which is now Texas, California, Utah, Nevada and parts of New Mexico, Arizona, Colorado, and Wyoming. Mexico overthrew Spain after 300 years, in 1821. In 1848 to end the Mexican War, Mexico agreed to cede the area now the above states to the U.S. in the Treaty of Guadalupe Hidalgo. The treaty guaranteed Mexicans' land rights, but these were not respected. Many Southwest Hispanics are descendants of area residents from the mid-1500s, and earlier, of course—if the indigenous lineage is considered. In the meantime, there have been immigrants from Central and South America and a steady flow from Mexico.

Spanish, the language of the conqueror, became the tongue of the occupied, as did the religion, Catholicism. In the New World, the Americas, all Hispanics are ultimately a mix of indigenous people and of Spanish conquerors. This mix is sometimes referred to, as "the new race," *la raza nueva,* or simply, *la raza.*

Early U.S. Hispanics came either from or through Mexico. This is important in this topic because, in addition to the old world Catholicism brought by the Spanish, the effect of Mexican Catholicism is also seen. In 1532 in what is presently Mexico City, history relates that there was the appearance of Mary, the mother of Jesus, to an Indian peasant, Juan Diego. Now known as Our Lady of Guadalupe, she appeared and directed him to continue being a good Catholic and attempted to influence as many of his fellows as possible toward that path. The Bishop did not believe that this humble Indian had indeed seen the Blessed Mother. She, however, knowing the doubt of the Bishop, miraculously produced and gave to Juan Diego, beautiful red roses in the dead of winter to prove to the Bishop that she indeed had appeared. Our Lady of Guadalupe continues to be a celebrated figure to most U.S. Hispanics in the Southwest, as in Mexico.

It is said by sociologists that the Mexican culture has overcome the fear of death. This is because much Mexican art depicts death, characterized by skeletons, in a playful manner, particularly around the day of all souls. There is indeed singing and poetry to death. This is one of the art and value issues that Americans know the most about. Indeed the Mexican culture, though it respects death, is acutely aware of its inevitability. The response is: because it is inevitable, to play with it, tease it, but continue to respect it.

Illness and Suffering:

Illness and suffering, regardless of genesis, are perceived as redemptive, consistent with the Catholic view of purgatory. This view holds that souls that are not condemned to hell because of dying, while in mortal (great) sin, have an opportunity to redeem other sins by suffering. For example, it is not unusual to hear of a suffering person, whether with cancer or an alcoholic spouse, or "ungrateful children," that the person has "already earned heaven."

When illness or injury is very serious, and particularly if the probability of death is perceived, Hispanics will frequently conduct what may appear to others as a "bribery" of a saint, including Our Lady of Guadalupe. This consists of a promise or contract with a particular saint, to fulfill a pilgrimage, specific prayers, or a novena (nine days of specific prayers), if the patient recovers. Pilgrimages are, in Mexico, most commonly to the basilica of our Lady of Guadalupe in Mexico City.

In northern New Mexico the most usual pilgrimage is to El Santuario de Nuestro Señor de Esquipulas in Chimayó, a small chapel for the child Jesus. Legend maintains that a farmer, instructed by a vision to dig beneath his plow for earth endowed with healing powers, uncovered a cross and a piece of cloth belonging to two priests martyred on the spot. The farmer placed the cross within a crude adobe chapel he built in 1816. The chapel is lined with cast-off crutches and braces discarded by patients who were cured by the healing earth. Some pilgrimages, both in Mexico City and in Chimayó, are promised and fulfilled through long walks, sometimes on the pilgrim's knees.

Promises like these are utilized, not only for recovery from illness, but also for other uncertainties, such as the return of a son from war or the survival of a marriage.

Visiting the Sick:
It is praiseworthy to visit the sick, particularly if

the effort required is great. During the visit, the patient—if speaking—or another close relative, will relate the promise contracted with a particular saint or Our Lady of Guadalupe, to fulfill a pilgrimage if recovery occurs.

Death:

For Catholic Hispanics, as for other Catholics, the Sacrament of the Sick is very important. Because of the history of rural living and the paucity of priests, however, many older Hispanic Catholics continue to view this rite as drastic and indicative of the proximity of death. This thinking is more in line with the older view by the Church, as the ritual was known as Extreme Unction. It is not rare, therefore, that a spouse or other family member may object to a priest administering the rite, as to them it may mean that death will soon follow. At these times, it may be helpful to ask the priest to explain that the rite is for the sick, not only for the dying.

Upon hearing news of a death, we do not hide our grief, sorrow, and pain. We generally unabashedly display our sorrow in front of others who, though they may be Catholic, do not as openly display these raw emotions. In the traditional, usually large Mexican American families, it is quite common to find family members who cry out loud when a death is announced. So great is the sorrow and the surrender to it that fainting is not unusual. There is open mourning around death and this is generally a rare time when men openly cry. With a death in the hospital, we generally disrupt the operations in the nursing unit.

Bereavement:

Sociologists who study bereavement report that the grieving process for Mexican Americans is much more effective and has less long-term mental health damage than with other groups who do not express as intensely.

Rituals:

In northern New Mexico rituals connected with the Catholic Church still persevere. The funeral mass is attended by the entire community, which generally walks with the bereaved from the church to the cemetery for the burial.

(Some families cover all mirrors in the house for various designated periods following a death. This however may be more indicative of the now-acknowledged history of many New Mexico families' descendency from "converted" Spanish Jews, *maranos,* who came to the new world at the time of the inquisition. In these families many Jewish practices tend to bleed with Catholic traditions, so that contemporary families cannot separate them).

Rituals and Afterlife:

Masses are said for the dead at one week, one month, six months, one year, two years, and five years. In more traditional families the women in the immediate family wear black clothes for a year. Masses and other prayers are offered in order to relieve the suffering that the soul would endure while in purgatory, before earning heaven. When the family has done all these things, they will feel that they have fulfilled their duties and can then move on.

Key Issues for Hospital and Hospice Personnel:

It is important to point out that although most Hispanics in the Southwest are Catholic by tradition, this is changing very rapidly. Many Protestants and the Mormon religion have recruited Hispanics, both in the U.S. and in Latin America, to fundamentalist Christian religions and the Church of the Latter Day Saints. Some Southwest observers now refer to the wave of Mormon conversions in the Southwest and Latin America as "the browning of Mormonism."

It is very important to check the official religion listed by a Hispanic American, and to call the respective pastor of that particular religion. Many converts to other religions have been known to revert back to the Catholic Church at the time of their anticipated death, but this must not be assumed. For this reason it is best to ask the patient himself/herself who they would want to be called.

It is critical to remember that all the family is notified and, depending on their roots with the tradition, all of them may report to the hospital to comfort the dying and each other. Restricting visitors may help or it may increase the grieving because the family is not able to see the patient.

Postmortem Attention:

Hispanics have no particular specific tradition for the postmortem stage. In most major U.S. cities with large populations of Hispanics, there is at least one funeral home owned or operated by a local

Hispanic; these funeral directors know the traditions and the variations. The family will probably select one of these.

Neither is there a particular specific tradition for autopsy or cadaver organ donation. If there is need for an autopsy, it should be carefully explained to the family in order to obtain free and informed consent.

More Hispanics are now knowledgeable of cadaver organ donation, though the donor numbers are still very low. This also should be explained. It will influence the family if they know who will be the recipient of their family member's organs.

Index